DATE DUE

EVALUATING
ART

EVALUATING ART

GEORGE DICKIE

Temple University Press
Philadelphia

Temple University Press, Philadelphia 19122
Copyright © 1988 by Temple University. All rights reserved
Published 1988
Printed in the United States of America

The paper used in this publication meets the minimum
requirements of American National Standard for Information
Sciences—Permanence of Paper for Printed Library Materials,
ANSI Z39.48-1984

Library of Congress Cataloging-in-Publication Data

Dickie, George, 1926–
Evaluating art.

Includes index.
1. Aesthetics. I. Title.
BH39.D493 1988 111'.85 88-29541
ISBN 0-87722-597-4

FOR SHANNAN

CONTENTS

PREFACE

In this book I present and argue for a theory of art evaluation. As far as I can tell this theory has no necessary connection with the institutional theory of art. This lack of connection should not be surprising, for the institutional theory of art is supposed to be a *classificatory* theory of art—a theory that explains why a work of art is a work of art. Why a work of art is valuable or disvaluable is an additional question.

I do not conceive of this book as a definitive solution to the theory of art evaluation. I conceive of it rather as occupying a middle position in the history of the topic. Monroe Beardsley and the other philosophers whose work is discussed here have made the important beginnings. I am trying to organize their insights, to get rid of what is wrong in their theories, to fill in gaps, and to work out a theory that is as adequate as I can make it at this time. I hope that this book will be useful to those who work on the theory of art evaluation in the future.

I thank Linda Andrews, David Brubaker, Andrzey Heyduk, Frank Youngwerth, and Professor Byung-nam Oh of Seoul National University, who were members of my 1985 graduate seminar in aesthetics and who studied with me the works of the philosophers whose writings are treated in this book. I thank Teresa Budziak, Joyce Carpenter, Bernard Conroy, Jennifer Faust, Paul Kindlon, William Lamp, and Abby Wilkerson, who were members of my 1986 graduate seminar in aesthetics and who read and criticized the first draft of this book. Special thanks are due Teresa Budziak, Joyce Carpenter, and William Lamp for their particularly forceful and useful criticisms. I thank David Owen, who was a member of my 1988 advanced undergraduate aesthetics course, for a useful comment on material from Chapter Nine.

I thank Professor Suzanne Cunningham of Loyola University of Chicago, Professor Marcia Eaton of the University of Minnesota, Professor Mark Johnson of Southern Illinois University, Professor Robert Yanal of Wayne State University, Anita Silvers of San Francisco State University, and two anonymous Temple University Press readers for comments on earlier drafts of this book. I thank Professor Ralf Meerbote of the University of Rochester for comments on an early version of Chapter Two.

Time to write the first draft of this book during 1985–1986 was made possible by a sabbatical leave granted by the University of Illinois at Chicago. Thanks are also due to the Institute for Advanced Studies in the Humanities at Edinburgh University, where I was a Fellow in the fall of 1985 and where earlier portions of the first draft were written.

Many of the ideas and arguments of Chapters Four and Six were originally worked out in "Evaluating Art," *British Journal of Aesthetics* 25 (Winter 1985): 3–16. Some of the ideas of Chapter Four were originally worked out in "Instrumental Inference," *Journal of Aesthetics and Art Criticism* 42 (Winter 1983): 151–154. Material from Chapter Two has appeared under the title "Hume's Way: The Path Not Taken" in *The Reasons of Art*, ed. Peter J. McCormick (Ottawa: University of Ottawa Press, 1985), pp. 309–314. Chapter Five in a slightly altered form appears in *The Journal of Aesthetics and Art Criticism* 46 (Winter 1987): 229–237 under the title "Beardsley, Sibley, and Critical Principles."

George Dickie
Chicago, Illinois

EVALUATING
ART

CHAPTER ONE

Introduction

David Hume begins "Of the Standard of Taste" by remarking at length on the diversity of taste. Is this diversity to be explained away, with some tastes seen as conforming to a universal standard and some tastes as deviating from it? Or is the diversity of taste, or some significant part of it, to be accepted as a datum? This question is the primary focus of this book. In other words, the primary concern of this book is the theory of normative art evaluation. Metalinguistic questions about the meaning of evaluational terms that have fascinated so many philosophers in recent times will be of little or no concern here.

It seems reasonable to approach theorizing about the evaluation of art by first outlining the possible theories of art evaluation—that is, the theories possible if the various traditional evaluative notions are used. I shall then see which of the possible theories can be set aside for large fatal reasons. The theories that remain will, of course, involve substantial difficulties or at least complexities of detail that must be dealt with in more subtle ways. After the field has been narrowed, I shall turn in Chapter Two to a discussion of the historical development of the theory of art evaluation. In Chapters Three through Nine, I shall examine critically the views of eight philosophers, trying to discover what can be derived from them and trying on this basis to work out a theory of art evaluation. These philosophers are, in the order in which I shall be discussing their views: Paul Ziff, Monroe Beardsley, Frank Sibley, Nelson Goodman, Nicholas Wolterstorff, David Hume, Bruce Vermazen, and J. O. Urmson. Each of these eight philosophers, in my opinion, has made a very important contribution of one kind or another to the theory of art evaluation, and, even if my efforts at theorizing on the subject are not successful, the examination of their views is in itself a worthwhile endeavour. There has not been as much theorizing about the evaluation of art as one might have expected. The work of the philosophers I shall be discussing seems to me to be the very best of that theorizing.

Of the philosophers discussed in this book only Beardsley has worked out an evaluational theory in detail. Consequently, it is Beardsley's theory that I shall use as a model and guide throughout this book, even though my views will diverge considerably from his.

The eight philosophers discussed here, as will emerge, sort out as hedgehogs and foxes, hedgehogs maintaining that the value of art resides in one large thing and foxes maintaining that the value of art is compounded of many different things. Beardsley and Goodman are hedgehogs; Ziff, Sibley, Wolterstorff, Vermazen, Urmson, and Hume are foxes. I shall run with the foxes. These philosophers, or at least some of them, also sort out in another way. Beardsley, Sibley, Vermazen, and, I think, Ziff conceive of aesthetic properties as the characteristics of art that are important for its evaluation. In this respect, these philosophers are in the tradition established by Schopenhauer. Goodman breaks sharply with the Schopenhauerian tradition in claiming that it is the cognitive features of art that are important for the evaluation of art. Wolterstorff and Hume believe that both aesthetic and cognitive features contribute to the value of art.

At this early point, there seem to be seven possible theories (or theory-types, for each can be filled in in slightly different ways to produce different theories). The theory-types appear to fall under four general headings: (A) imitation value theory, (B) objective intrinsic value theories, (C) subjective intrinsic value theory, and (D) instrumental value theories. With ingenuity the number of headings could be reduced to three, but such rigor is not necessary at this point.

Possible Theories: Types of Artistic Value

A. Imitation Value Theory
   1. Works of art are valuable because they imitate or represent aspects of the world.

B. Objective Intrinsic Value Theories
   2. Works of art are valuable because they possess the one and only objective intrinsic value property in some degree.

   3. Works of art are valuable because they possess one or more of several objective intrinsic value properties in some degree.

C. Subjective Intrinsic Value Theory
   4. Works of art are valuable because they are intrinsically valued by some person or persons. ("Intrinsically valuing" is to be understood here as contrasting with valuing something because of its consequences.)

D. Instrumental Value Theories
   5. Works of art are valuable because they can be the instrumental source of a valuable experience that in turn is valuable because the experience or an element of it is intrinsically valued by some person or persons.

   6. Works of art are valuable because they can be the instrumental source of a valuable experience that in turn is valuable because the experience or an element of it is instrumentally valuable.

7. Works of art are valuable because they can be the instrumental source of a valuable experience that in turn is valuable because the experience or an element of it is intrinsically valued by some person or persons and/or the experience or an element of it is instrumentally valuable.

As a general theory, the imitation value theory will clearly not do. There are just too many nonrepresentational works of art. Furthermore, even representational works have valuable aspects that are not representational. Nevertheless, so many people over so long a time have admired the representational features of art that it would be a mistake to wholly ignore them. What is of value in this theory can be incorporated into a more promising theory at a later point.

The objective intrinsic value theory-types can be set aside for epistemological reasons: the kind of value features involved in these theory-types require, as they are usually thought of, a special nonempirical status and a special epistemological way of knowing them. Works of art and other things may have such value properties but the difficulties involved in coming to know such properties make theories that refer to them unattractive and unworkable. Since I am setting aside the notion of objective intrinsic value properties, I have not bothered to formulate as possible theory-types those combination theory-types that would involve objective intrinsic properties.

Theory-type number 4, the view that works of art are valuable because they are intrinsically valued by some person or persons, has a certain plausibility. But I think it gets what plausibility it has because it is easily confused with the more plausible theory-type number 5. Theory-type number 4 asserts that it is works of art themselves that are intrinsically valued, while theory-type number 5 asserts that it is the *experiences* of which works of art are the source that are intrinsically valued. The plausibility of theory-type number 5 no doubt rests on the fact that there have been so many instances of theories that fit or seem to fit this mold; for example, eighteenth-century theories of taste hold pleasure to be the intrinsically valued state of mind and many of the later aesthetic theories hold aesthetic experience to be the intrinsically valued state of mind. We have thus become used to thinking about intrinsically valuing states of mind. But theory-type number 4 asserts that it is the works of art themselves that can be intrinsically valued rather than the experiences generated by them and this seems odd. There is of course no terrible defect such as inconsistency in theory-type number 4 nor any epistemological problem as with the objective intrinsic theory-types, just an oddness about what is supposed to be intrinsically valued. Furthermore, there do not seem to have been any historical instances of this kind of theory-type. I set theory-type number 4 aside without actually having defeated it or without perhaps even damaging it very seriously. But it certainly seems to lack promise.

The three theory-types that remain are all instrumentalist:

5. Works of art are valuable because they can be the instrumental source of a valuable experience that in turn is valuable because the experience or an element of it is intrinsically valued by some person or persons.

6. Works of art are valuable because they can be the instrumental source of a valuable experience that in turn is valuable because the experience or an element of it is instrumentally valuable.

7. Works of art are valuable because they can be the instrumental source of a valuable experience that in turn is valuable because the experience or an element of it is intrinsically valued by some person or persons and/or the experience or an element of it is instrumentally valuable.

These three instrumentalist theory-types can be diagrammed as shown in Figure 1.

Instrumentalist theory-types have certain advantages. Both num-

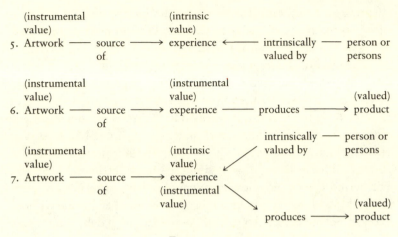

F I G U R E   I

ber 5 and number 7 make use of the notion of intrinsic valuing, and we do in fact intrinsically value and disvalue some experiences, so the notion is intelligible to us and usable by us. Of course, it may turn out that intrinsically valuing does not have any application to the product or products of works of art. Indeed, if Monroe Beardsley's account of art evaluation, which is an instance of theory-type 6, is correct, intrinsic valuing does not have such an application.

All three of the instrumentalist theory-types have the advantage that they make use of the notion of instrumental valuing, and we do in fact instrumentally value some things and experiences; so the notion is intelligible to us and usable by us. Of course, it may turn out that instrumentally valuing does not have any application to works of art as required by all three theory-types or to the product or products of works of art as required by theory-types 6 and 7.

The instrumentalist theory-types have another advantage. Even the most rudimentary reflection on the kind of things that works of art are indicates that they are the kind of thing that are the source of and are used as a source of valuable experience and that they are created to serve this purpose.

8

But if the instrumentalist theory-types have advantages over the other theory-types, there are a number of problems that they must confront, some of which derive from the history of philosophizing about the value of art. It was easy enough to set aside the theory-types that involve objective intrinsic value properties, but it is not so easy to set aside the great influence of such theories. Objective intrinsic theory has been particularly influential and has embedded itself in the minds of philosophers and the general public as the model of what the theory of art evaluation ought to be and do. Even those who have rejected this theory of art evaluation have been influenced by it, so that for later theorists this theory has set the problems and the expectations of how those problems must be solved. The influential view I am concerned with had its origins in the philosophy of Plato, especially his theory of beauty, but the objective intrinsic theory of art evaluation was not of course held by Plato, and I am not attributing it to him. Plato himself was not so much concerned with the evaluation of works of art as with the devaluating of the whole art enterprise.

Consider some of the specific influences of the objective intrinsic theory. This theory claims that there is one and only one objective artistic value property (beauty) and that works of art and other things can possess this property in varying degrees. If an object has some particular degree of beauty, then its degree of beauty is subject to some kind of measurement, at least an estimate of an informal kind. If an object's degree of beauty can be estimated, then objects possessing beauty can be compared as to whether they are equal in beauty or of greater or lesser beauty, at least within certain limits. Subsequent theorizing about the evaluation of art has taken it as a set piece to show how the value of works of art can be measured and, consequently, how works can be compared and ranked with regard to their value.

Also, on this influential view, if two persons disagree about whether an object possesses beauty or about the degree of an object's beauty, one or both of them must be wrong, for beauty is supposed to be an objective property. For this view, the question of relativism does not arise; that is, it is not theoretically possible for two persons to disagree about the value of a work of art and for at least one of them not to be wrong. Much subsequent theorizing about art evaluation has taken as a set piece that relativism must be avoided. Kant's oft-quoted remark about speaking with a universal voice demanding agreement with one's judgments of taste is an eighteenth-century echo of the view I have been discussing.

One problem that the influential view does not resolve, although it may give the appearance of doing so, is that of accounting for specific evaluations. On this view, it is easy enough to see that an object may possess beauty in small degree or middling degree or great degree. But when does an object possess enough beauty to be beautiful? Or when does an object possess so little beauty that it is ugly? An object can possess beauty without being beautiful or ugly. The question is, What degree of beauty is required to make an object have a specific value? Although this theory shows how art could have *value,* it does not resolve the problem of specific artistic evaluations—the problem of knowing when, as we would now say, art is good, bad, or mediocre.

There are, then, a number of problems that each of the three instrumentalist theory-types of art evaluation must face. First, all three, as any account of art evaluation would, face the problem of how to provide a place for an account of specific evaluations: bad art, mediocre art, good art, excellent art, and so on. Each theory-type, as stated, is an account of artistic *value,* and to show how art has value is one thing, but to show how works can have specific values (that is, bad, mediocre, good, and the like) is an additional task.

Second, in theory-types 5 and 7 a person or persons as intrinsically valuing are explicitly mentioned, and this raises the problem of what kind of person or persons do the valuing; that is to say, it raises the problem of relativism because persons can and do disagree in their valuing. Relativism has been recognized as a problem for the evaluation of art for a very long time. Other theorists have grappled with relativism, but David Hume makes a sustained and sophisticated attempt to deal with it. Hume tries to specify the characteristics of the ideal person to experience the pleasure of taste. As it turns out, however, Hume does not, nor does he really attempt to, completely avoid relativism. Any theory that employs the notion of persons in a central way must have some means of dealing with relativism—either by following Hume's lead or by developing some other strategy.

In theory-type 6, persons are not explicitly referred to, but of course with such theories it is the experience of persons that is envisaged as the experience of a work of art. But at least in the theory of Beardsley, whose view is an instance of type 6, the problem of persons "washes out," because although it is the aesthetic experience of a person that is valuable, the value that aesthetic experience has, according to Beardsley, is also instrumental value and therefore is not the intrinsic valuing of a person or persons. Beardsley by this strategy avoids relativism, but his way is quite different from Hume's ideal judge approach.

The eight philosophers who have made such important contributions to the theory of art evaluation and with whom I shall be concerned from Chapter Three through the end of the book are all instrumentalists of one kind or another. I regard this as a powerful indication that instrumentalism is the route to travel.

In commenting earlier on the imitation value theory, I acknowledged the value significance of representational features of art. The rejection of representation and the other cognitive features of art as artistic values is, however, a prominent feature of many present-day evaluation theories. Why is this so? The answer is that philosophical views worked out in the late eighteenth and early nineteenth centuries undermined representation and the other cognitive dimensions of art as artistic values. So before turning to the theories of present-day philosophers, I shall, in the next chapter, examine the ways in which eighteenth-century and nineteenth-century philosophers treated representation in their evaluational theories.

Turning to present-day philosophers, in Chapter Three, I shall examine the view of Paul Ziff as it is expressed in his article "Reasons in Art Criticism." In the relatively short space of an article, Ziff attempts to set out the core aspects of a complete evaluational theory. An examination of this article enables me to get before the reader quickly an account of many of the major aspects of the theory of art evaluation—critical principles and reasons, relativism, and instrumentalism itself. In addition, in the course of my critical examination of Ziff's theory, I raise an issue that becomes a persistent theme of my book, namely, the distinction between what I shall subsequently call "strong principles" and "weak principles" of artistic criticism. Strong principles are principles that claim to involve strong, specific, evaluational predicates such as "is good," "is poor," "is bad," and the like. Weak principles are principles that involve weak, nonspecific, evaluational predicates such as "has value," "has some degree of goodness," and the like. And, of course, in addition, Ziff has many insightful and stimulating things to say about the evaluation of art.

In Chapter Four and the first part of Chapter Five, I shall examine Monroe Beardsley's theory of art evaluation in extensive detail. As noted earlier, throughout this book I shall in various ways be using Beardsley's theory as guide. Despite some fundamental disagreements with his theory, I regard it as an enormous philosophical achievement. It is a complete theory—perhaps the first complete theory ever formulated. Furthermore, it is worked out in very great detail. It is impossible to work on the theory of art evaluation without going through Beardsley's theory, for he has marked all the trails and taken us a good ways down almost all of them.

In the second part of Chapter Five, I shall focus on the criticism of Beardsley's theory contained in Frank Sibley's article "General Criteria and Reasons in Aesthetics." Sibley's brilliant insight into a difficulty involved in Beardsley's account of critical principles makes possible the formulation of a more accurate account of such principles. I also argue that Sibley is mistaken in some of his criticisms of elements of Beardsley's theory. At the end of this chapter, I arrive at what I call "the compromise view" of critical principles, which involves the sacrificing of some of both Beardsley's theory and Sibley's conclusions.

In Chapter Six, I discuss the cognitivist theory of art evaluation sketched out by Nelson Goodman in *Languages of Art* and elsewhere. I also examine the controversy between Beardsley and Goodman over the nature of artistic value and the nature of the proper experience of art. Goodman argues that art's value is cognitive value, which art achieves by referring to aspects of the world. Beardsley argues that art's value is not cognitive but is value art derives from its capacity to produce detached experience, which nullifies any reference a work of art makes to the world. I argue that both Beardsley and Goodman have over-generalized, but that something can be gleaned from each. At the end of this chapter, I arrive at what I call "the amplified, compromise view."

In Chapter Seven, I continue to amplify the compromise view by examining Nicholas Wolterstorff's remarks on the evaluation of art in his book *Art in Action*. Wolterstorff's remarks constitute a refinement of Goodman's rather sketchily outlined account of the cognitive value of art. But unlike Goodman, Wolterstorff acknowledges the artistic value of aesthetic qualities. I go on to examine the relationship between the cognitive and aesthetic characteristics of art and to examine the dynamics of the experiences of art that involve both cognitive and aesthetic features. I also discuss the question of the artistic value of the moral content in works of art.

In Chapter Eight, I address the question of how the various evaluational theories already discussed deal with the problem of relativism. I then develop my own view of relativism through an analysis of David Hume's "Of the Standard of Taste."

Chapter Nine has as its two-fold goal the development of an account that will allow for value comparisons among works of art and for specific, strong evaluations ("X is good," "X is bad," and the like). It has been a traditional philosophical desire that a theory of art evaluation should provide a foundation that will allow for the comparison of the value of every work of art with the value of every other work of art. Beardsley's theory, for example, is supposed to provide such a foundation. Using the account worked out by Bruce Vermazen in "Comparing Evaluations of Works of Art" as a basis, I develop a scheme for limited comparisons of evaluations of works of art. This scheme does not satisfy the traditional philosophical desire for unlimited comparisons, which I regard as unrealistic. Working within the scheme of limited comparisons of the evaluations of works of art and following the lead of J. O. Urmson's "On Grading," I work out an account that shows how strong, specific evaluations of works of art are made.

CHAPTER TWO

The Historical Background

One of the most remarkable and relatively recent changes in the way that philosophers theorize about the evaluation of art has been the rejection of the representative or more generally the cognitive element as being of artistic value. Plato long ago of course denigrated the value of the representation in art of the world of sights and sounds, but his view is generally regarded as idiosyncratic and merely curious. Aristotle in contrast uses imitation (representation) as one of the criteria of artistic value. Imitation establishes a powerful relation between art and the world it represents. The great majority of humankind from Aristotle's day to the present has agreed with him that imitation is artistically valuable, and so have most philosophers until relatively recently. The conventional wisdom of the dominant, present-day philosophical theorizing about the evaluation of art, however, denies the importance of representation and other cognitive elements that relate art to the world and thereby denies the significance of the relation between art and the rest of life. Beardsley's theory is a prime example of this negative attitude toward the artistic value of the cognitive aspects of art, but many of the views that will be discussed in the following chapters also exhibit this same attitude. How has this relatively recent change come about?

The explanation of the change in the value status of the representational and cognitive elements generally in art must begin with an examination of the views of certain eighteenth-century philosophers. The attempt to develop theories to explain the experience of art and to justify the evaluating of art did not begin in the eighteenth century, but a *new* beginning was made early in that century with the advent of the theory of taste. An enormous number of different theories of taste appeared during the eighteenth century. The artistic value of representation or imitation in the experience of art was acknowledged in one way or another by these theories, so it was not the theory of taste as such that did in imitation. It was Kant's theory of taste, especially as understood by Schopenhauer, that sealed the fate of imitation, denying it a role in the proper experience of art. Or rather, it was one aspect of Kant's theory of taste, the aspect that so influenced Schopenhauer, that sealed the fate of imitation. Kant made a technical adjustment in the notion of the faculty taste and thereby altered the course of aesthetic theory. Kant did not himself reject imitation as unimportant—at least in the later part of "The Critique of Aesthetic Judgement," although perhaps he should have in order to be consistent with its earlier part. In any event, it was the earlier part that influenced Schopenhauer and thereby helped determine the dominant view, and insofar as the dominant view is concerned, imitation is not an artistic value. (In the remainder of this chapter, when I refer to Kant's theory of taste, I shall be referring to the influential earlier part.)

In this chapter, I shall discuss the theories of taste of Shaftesbury, Francis Hutcheson, Edmund Burke, Hume, and Kant, because all of these theories are important in the line of historical development I am tracing. I shall also discuss Schopenhauer's aesthetic theory, which as noted absorbed the relevant Kantian notion and embedded it in modern philosophical thought.

The notion of the disinterestedness of the experience of beauty plays a central role in each of the theories of taste and in Schopenhauer's aesthetic theory also. In the earlier theories of taste, the disinterestedness of the experience of beauty involves no necessary conflict between the experience of a beautiful art object and the experience of representational (imitative) features of that art object. With Kant's alteration in the theory of taste and the consequent enormous expansion of the scope of disinterestedness in his and Schopenhauer's theories, it became the dominant view that there is a necessary conflict between the experience of a beautiful art object and its representational features.

In what follows, I shall trace the idea of disinterestedness from its introduction into theorizing about beauty in theories of taste to Schopenhauer's theory, which has been so influential on present-day theories of aesthetic experience. As is well known, disinterestedness was brought into the theorizing about beauty by Shaftesbury. What is not well known or recognized is that the form that disinterestedness takes in the theories of Shaftesbury and his more immediate followers is very different from the form it takes in the aspect of Kant's theory of taste with which I am concerned and in theories subsequent to Kant. In the earlier theories of taste, the disinterestedness of the experience of a beautiful object is compatible with the experiencing at the same time of the representational (imitative) features of that object, if it has any. In the later theories, the disinterestedness of the experience of a beautiful object is held to be incompatible with and to prevent the experiencing at the same time of the representational features of that object. For the later theories, when the object in question is a work of art, only its beauty (for present-day theories read aesthetic qualities, for example, unity, delicacy, gracefulness, and the like) can be experienced in a proper experience of the art and, consequently, only art's beauty (or aesthetic qualities) and none of its imitative features count in evaluating art.

Shaftesbury introduced the notion of disinterestedness into the theory of the experience of beauty as a part of his attempt to counter the Hobbesian idea that all action and approbation is selfish, that is, always involves the calculation of anticipated benefit where either action or approbation are concerned. Shaftesbury argues against the "self-love" theory by producing what he thinks are clear counter-examples. The first example he mentions does not involve the arts at all but rather the experience of doing or thinking about mathematics. If we reflect on the pleasure we take in doing mathematics, "we shall find it of a kind which relates not in the least to any private interest . . . , nor has for its object any self-good or advantage of the private system. The admiration, joy, or love turns wholly upon what is exterior and foreign to ourselves."[1] Shaftesbury's point is that the basic pleasure we derive from an activity is not self-interested and is independent of calculation or anticipation; that is, we just enjoy the activity of doing mathematics independently of whether it promises future pleasure. Of course, once we discover that an activity gives pleasure, we can make use of this information to anticipate and calculate benefit. Shaftesbury's point can be illustrated by considering the following two different kinds of pleasure: (1) the present interested pleasure one might take today in anticipating the future pleasure of doing mathematics tomorrow and (2) the anticipated and noninterested future pleasure of doing mathematics tomorrow. That these are two distinct pleasures is clearly shown by the facts (1) that the present interested pleasure can occur and the future disinterested pleasure can fail to occur and (2) that the disinterested pleasure can occur without being anticipated. The occurrence of a disinterested pleasure in doing mathematics is sufficient to refute the Hobbesian claim that all activity is selfish, that is, that all approbation and action is motivated by anticipated pleasure or pain.

At a later point in his book, Shaftesbury discusses four examples of the pleasure taken in the experience of beauty that are analogous to the mathematical example, and it is at this point that he introduces the notion of disinterestedness into the theory of taste. In the first case, Shaftesbury contrasts the enjoyment of contemplating the beauty of the ocean with the enjoyment of owning the ocean. Shaftesbury remarks that the enjoyment of ownership is "very different from that which should naturally follow from contemplation of the ocean's beauty."[2] He is here making the same point that he makes in the passage about the mathematical proof, namely, that two different enjoyments (a nonselfish one and a selfish one) are involved in this kind of case. In the second case, Shaftesbury asks a question about the contemplation of a tract of land and the ownership of the land. He asks if one "should, for the enjoyment of the prospect, require the property or possession of the land."[3] The answer is, "No," because one can look at and nonselfishly enjoy contemplating the tract without owning it. The next two cases also involve distinguishing the enjoyment of the contemplation of beauty from the enjoyment of anticipated benefit, but in these two last cases there is also a suggestion of conflict between the two enjoyments. The third case involves distinguishing between the enjoyment of the contemplation of the beauty of a grove of trees and the enjoyment of the eating of the fruit of the trees. Shaftesbury suggests that the actual or anticipated enjoyment of the fruit may divert one from the beauty of the grove. And so it may, if one is very hungry. The fourth case involves distinguishing between the enjoyment of contemplating human beauty and desire for sexual possession. Shaftesbury suggests that the "eager desires, wishes, and hopes" for sexual possession are "no way suitable . . . to [the] rational and refined contemplation of beauty."[4] He is saying that the desire for sexual possession may crowd out the contemplation of human beauty. And so it may. Shaftesbury is free, however, to agree with Edmund Burke's later remark that "desire may sometimes operate along with" the appreciation of human beauty,[5] although Shaftesbury gives the impression of being less optimistic than Burke is that this will happen with great frequency. There is, however, nothing in Shaftesbury's (or Burke's) view that makes the conflict between the disinterested pleasure of contemplating human beauty and the interested pleasure of desiring sexual possession a necessary conflict. Consequently, no theoretical mental machinery is required by Shaftesbury (or Burke) to eliminate a necessary conflict. For these two thinkers, there is no necessary conflict between the disinterestedness of an experience of beauty and any interest that may attach itself to it.

Shaftesbury's cases are concerned with only one kind of relation —the relation between an object of a present experience and an anticipated future benefit. His cases do not raise the question of the significance of the referential relation involved in imitation.

Francis Hutcheson, following Shaftesbury, holds that the experience of beauty is disinterested, but whereas Shaftesbury's remarks are restricted to producing counterexamples, Hutcheson works out a complex theory to explain why this is so.[6] Thus, like Shaftesbury, Hutcheson is concerned with the question of the relation between an object of a present experience and an anticipated future benefit, but he also makes some attempt to come to grips with the referential relation involved in imitation.

In addition to the cognitive senses—vision, hearing, and the like —there are, according to Hutcheson, reflex senses such as the moral sense and the sense of beauty. These reflex senses are not cognitive, that is, not means of knowing aspects of the external world, but reactive; that is, these senses react to produce pleasure or pain when the cognitive senses inform a person that certain specific states of affairs obtain in the world. The sense of beauty, according to Hutcheson, reacts to produce pleasure when the cognitive senses cause a person to be aware of uniformity in variety.

There are four standard features of all theories of taste: (1) the cognitive faculties, (2) a faculty of taste, (3) an object of taste, and (4) pleasure. Different theorists give different accounts of the standard features. For Hutcheson, the "fit" between the sense of beauty (the faculty of taste) and its object (uniformity in variety) is specific: this reflex sense can be triggered only by uniformity in variety. This specific "fit" explains why the experience of beauty is disinterested:

if the sense of beauty can respond only to uniformity in variety, it is immune to the influence of any anticipated benefit. Moreover, the response of the sense of beauty is supposed to be involuntary and unmediated and, hence, not subject to influence. An analogous case with the cognitive sense of vision would be the seeing of a red object: no interest of a person in an anticipated benefit under any sort of normal conditions could cause that person to see the object as anything but red.

This, then, is the way that Hutcheson's theory deals with the question of a beautiful object's relation to anticipated benefit: he denies that such a relation is relevant to the object's beauty. But what of the other relations that a beautiful object may have—for example, a referential relation when the beautiful object is a representation? Consider two kinds of cases: a beautiful object that is not a representation and one that is.

Consider first the description that Hutcheson's theory entails of the experience of a beautiful object when the object is one that contains no references to anything outside it, say, a nonobjective painting or a typical piece of instrumental music. Using the cognitive senses (vision or hearing), a person becomes aware of the elements and structure of the painting or the music and, consequently, of uniformity in variety in the experience of the object. Since in the kinds of cases under discussion, there are no references to things outside the works, the only things on which uniformity in variety can depend are the elements and structure "inside" the works themselves.

But consider now the description that Hutcheson's theory entails of the experience of a beautiful object when the object is a literary work that makes references to the actual world—for example, *War and Peace*. Using the cognitive senses (reading), a person becomes aware of the content of the novel and, consequently, of uniformity in variety in the experience of the novel. The uniformity can derive from various sources internal to the novel: character consistency, overall theme, and other aspects that involve similarity among elements. When, however, a work of art represents an aspect of the actual world, uniformity in the experience can come, according to Hutcheson, from the similarity between the representation and the actual thing represented. In *War and Peace*, this second source of uniformity in the experience of the novel can come, for example, from the similarity between the representation of Napoleon in the novel and the actual historical Napoleon.

In such cases, the object of taste is not the referential features of the work of art itself but the more complex object consisting of (1) those referential features of the work of art, (2) what is represented, and (3) the resemblance relation between the two. The uniformity of this more complex object is what interacts with the sense of beauty. Thus, in these cases, the object of taste itself (which interacts with the sense of beauty) is not referential, although it contains a referential relation and both of its terms (the referential features of the work of art and what it refers to). (Note that for Hutcheson representation turns out to be an element of uniformity that depends upon the similarity between an element of the work of art and something outside of the work of art. Representation so construed interacts in a kind of indirect way with the sense of beauty.) Once the various uniformities in variety are noticed, the sense of beauty is triggered and pleasure is produced. There is, however, for Hutcheson, nothing about the nature of the faculty of taste that prevents it from having been directly reactive to referentiality or anything else; God could have made us so.

The experience of *War and Peace* is disinterested, on Hutcheson's theory, because only the perceived uniformity in variety can trigger the sense of beauty, but the experience of the novel is not segregated from the actual world or the rest of experience. Indeed, the experience of a work such as *War and Peace* actively involves relating aspects of it to the actual world, and, furthermore, according to Hutcheson's theory, the more accurate the representations are of the represented things in the actual world, the more perceived uniformity there is in the experience. Hutcheson "buries" the representation or reference that occurs in art within the object of taste. The representational aspect of a work of art and the thing referred to become, for Hutcheson, two terms of a unity relation. Thus, the object of taste—uniformity in variety—swallows up the referentiality. The representationality of art, for Hutcheson, cannot be independently valuable. In Hutcheson's later and less influential writings, he speaks of a sense of imitation as well as a sense of beauty; such an additional sense would take pleasure directly in imitation and independently of the sense of beauty. On this later view, referentiality would not be "buried" in uniformity in variety.[7]

For Hutcheson the faculty of taste and the cognitive faculties are conceived of as entirely different mental structures. Hutcheson refers to the cognitive faculties as the external senses (they relate the mind to the external world), and he refers to the sense of beauty as an internal, reflex sense. The cognitive faculties occupy a "forward" position in the mind; that is, they are required to bring information into the mind. The faculty of taste occupies a "rear" position in the mind; in the mental process that underlies the experience of beauty, the sense of beauty is the last thing to function. For Hutcheson, the cognitive faculties function in the same way in both the experiences of beauty and in all other experiences. What distinguishes the experiences of beauty from other experiences is that in experiences of beauty the faculty of taste is triggered and produces pleasure. Thus, for Hutcheson, works of art (as objects of beauty) are experienced cognitively in the same way as other objects. The disinterestedness of the faculty of taste in Hutcheson's theory does not cut off the object of taste from its relations to the rest of experience. (See Figure 2 for Hutcheson's conceptions of what goes on in the mind during the experiences of a beautiful object and of an ordinary object.)

Edmund Burke's theory of taste is in the Hutchesonian mold, although it differs in several important respects from Hutcheson's view. Burke denies that there is a special sense of beauty that consti-

Ordinary experience

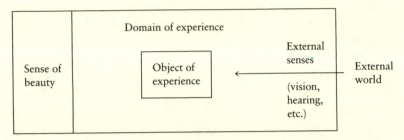

Experience of beauty

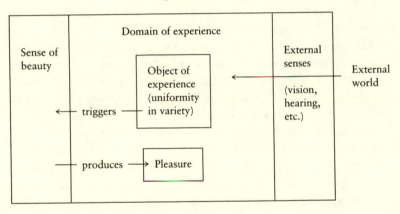

FIGURE 2

For Hutcheson, in both the cases of ordinary experience and the experience of beauty stimulation comes into the mind from the external world and becomes the object of experience. In the experience of beauty, the uniformity in variety of an object of experience triggers the faculty of taste and produces pleasure.

tutes the faculty of taste; he claims that the human constitution just reacts to certain specific features of the world with pleasure or pain. So Burke is not very specific about the nature of the faculty of taste. Nevertheless, Burke agrees that the experience of beauty is disinterested. He disagrees with Hutcheson that there is a single property such as uniformity in variety that triggers the faculty of taste where beauty is concerned; Burke maintains that there is a "short list" of properties that characterize beautiful objects—smallness, smoothness, deviating insensibly from a right line, and the like. None of the properties on Burke's beauty list involves representation. But Burke, like the later Hutcheson, asserts that imitation does cause pleasure. So Burke's theory does not exclude the representational features of beautiful objects from the experience of those objects.

Hume's theory of taste is also in the Hutchesonian mold, but he is more cautious and less metaphysically speculative than Hutcheson.[8] Hume slyly avoids any explicit or detailed characterization of the faculty of taste, although what he does say makes clear that he conceives of it in the Hutchesonian manner as a reflex, in-the-"rear"-of-the-mind sort of affair. Hume's view of objects of taste, however, is strikingly different from Hutcheson's. Hume makes no attempt at all to follow Hutcheson and try to discover a neat, single characteristic such as uniformity in variety that triggers the faculty of taste. Hume does not even try the "short-list" approach of Burke —smoothness, smallness, and the like. In fact, in "Of the Standard of Taste," I count thirty-three descriptions of things that Hume mentions as either pleasing or displeasing to taste, and it is clear that these descriptions are not intended as a complete list.

Of these thirty-three descriptions, eleven seem to be different ways of referring to uniformity and two of them ways of referring to variety, so Hume is partially following Hutcheson. This leaves, however, twenty non-Hutchesonian characteristics. Some of the twenty are similar to those on Burke's beauty short list in that they are nonrepresentational: for example, "force and clearness of . . . expression," "lustre of colours," harshness, and the like. But many of the characteristics he mentions throughout are representational: for example, "natural pictures of the passions," "exactness of imitation," and "amorous and tender images," and he makes no attempt to subsume these neatly under uniformity as the early Hutcheson does. When Hume speaks of "natural pictures of the passions" and "exactness of imitation" as beauties, he is clearly saying that such representational features of works of art are valuable because they are accurate representations and not because they are aspects of some more general characteristic such as uniformity in variety. Hume's view here is similar to that of the later Hutcheson and Burke, although Hume does not speculate about a sense of imitation as Hutcheson does. And Hume makes no attempt to develop separate accounts of beauty, the sublime, imitation, and the like, as Burke, Hutcheson, and others do; he just gives a long, incomplete list of characteristics that cause pleasure or pain.

Near the end of the essay Hume makes a remark of particular interest. He writes, "But where the ideas of morality and decency alter from one age to another, and where vicious manners are described, without being marked with the proper characters of blame and disapprobation, this must be allowed to disfigure the poem, and to be a real deformity."[9] And at the end of the essay, Hume remarks that Roman Catholic "bigotry has disfigured two very fine tragedies of the French theatre, *Polieucte* and *Athalia*; where an intemperate zeal for particular modes of worship is set off with all the pomp imaginable, and forms the predominant character of the heroes." Hume quotes a passage from one of the plays to illustrate the religious bigotry that disfigures it: " 'What is this,' says the sublime Joad to Josabet, finding her in discourse with Mathan, the priest of Baal, 'Does the daughter of David speak to this traitor? . . . Why comes that enemy of God hither to poison the air, which we breathe, with his horrid presence?' "[10]

The early Hutcheson would say that an inaccurate imitation is a defect because it produces disunity, but Hume is not saying that in the passage just quoted. The later Hutcheson who speaks of a sense of imitation would say that a bad imitation is a defect because it displeases the sense of imitation, but Hume is not saying that either. Hume is saying that the play is defective because it is a representation of a morally bad state of affairs and nothing in the play condemns this morally bad state of affairs. There are for Hume two ways in which imitation can be involved in artistic value: (1) the accuracy of imitation and (2) the imitation of a thing that has moral value or disvalue.

The view of imitation of these British theorists of taste is clear. They are not theoretically surprised to find references to the world and its morality in works of art. Such referentiality in art is for them a perfectly natural thing that may have important consequences for the value of the art in which it occurs. For them, referentiality in art is not something to be conjured away, and in fact they work out ways to deal with it within their theories. They are free to see works of art as they are and to deal with them as they are. If aesthetics had followed them, the history of aesthetics would have been very different. Unfortunately, the history of aesthetics followed Kant, or rather the early part of "The Critique of Aesthetic Judgement," and Schopenhauer.

In the following discussion of Kant's view, I shall be concerned only with his theory of judgments of taste, that is, with his conception of beauty, which is given in the early part of "The Critique of Aesthetic Judgement." I shall be concerned with the implications of Kant's account of judgments of taste for the experience of art. I shall ignore what Kant says about art in the later part of "The Critique of Aesthetic Judgement," since it does not seem to have influenced Schopenhauer and because it does not appear to be consistent with his theory of judgments of taste.

Kant's theory of taste is clearly in the same line of development as Hutcheson's and Burke's, but his conception of the nature of the

faculty of taste greatly expands the scope and power of disinterestedness in his theory. Consider this well-known passage from the "First
Moment" of the "Analytic of the Beautiful."

> The delight which we connect with the representation of the real
> existence of an object is called interest. Such a delight, therefore,
> always involves a reference to the faculty of desire. . . . Now
> where the question is whether something is beautiful, we do not
> want to know, whether we, or any one else, are, or even could
> be, concerned in the real existence of the thing, but rather what
> estimate we form of it on mere contemplation.[11]

When Kant speaks of the real existence of an object, he means, at
least, that a series of actual or possible experiences cohere through
time. For example, if the book before me is real, I can have a series
of similar experiences through time. Thus, real existence involves a
series of experiences that stand in certain relations to one another.
Experiences that lack these relations are illusory. An object's real
existence involves it in relations to other objects and in relations to
its own future and past states, and it is through these relations that
desire, that is, interest, can get a foothold; it is through an object's
relation to some actual or possible experience that desire can arise
by anticipating a future beneficial experience. When Kant claims
that the beautiful object has no involvement with real existence, he
is saying that the object's being beautiful does not involve having
relations to anything else. The beautiful object can, as a result, involve no reference to desire. When Kant says in his convoluted way
that, when the question is whether something is beautiful, we are
not concerned with the real existence of the thing, he means that we
are concerned only with the present object in experience independent of its relations to other things. This sounds very much like what
Hutcheson says, but the object of experience is being conceived of by
the two thinkers in very different ways. Hutcheson is thinking of the
object of the experience in a comparatively ordinary way as, say, a

physical object with a certain degree of uniformity in variety. Kant, however, is conceiving of the object of the experience as an appearance at a given time, not as a full-blown physical object, that is, not as something with real existence. Kant, in connecting real existence with the notion of disinterestedness, introduces an additional kind of isolation to the object of the experience of beauty. This difference between the Hutchesonian view and the Kantian one may not sound very significant, but it opens up the possibility for an interpretation of Kant's view that results in a very great difference between the two theories. If the Kantian position is understood in a certain way, the result is the view that a beautiful object is experientially cut off from everything else. On this interpretation, for Kant, the disinterestedness of beauty is achieved by isolating the experience of beauty from any anticipated future benefit, and in doing this the beautiful object is isolated from everything else it stands in relation to, including anything it might represent.

To further illustrate the meaning of the quoted passage for this interpretation, let me describe a simple perceptual situation, say, looking at a beautiful painting. If I have an experience of the painting now, for all I know the experience may be illusory, that is, may not be of a thing that has real existence. If, however, I have similar experiences over a period of time, I will attribute real existence to the painting—the present experience and similar experiences yesterday and the day before allow me to conclude that there is a real physical painting that persists through time. The present appearance and the earlier appearances stand in a relationship that establishes the existence of a physical object. For Kant, when we are concerned with the beauty of the painting, we are and only can be concerned with a present object independent of its relations to other things. In addition, on this interpretation the experience of the beautiful painting is experientially cut off from everything else; its relations to other appearances are experientially nullified. Such a disinterested experience is in some respects like an illusory experience.

The explanation of why, on this interpretation of Kant's theory, a beautiful object—whether natural object or work of art—is experientially isolated lies in Kant's conception of the faculty of taste. As noted earlier, Hutcheson conceives of the faculty of taste as a reflex sense, that, so to speak, is located at the "rear" of the mind. For Hutcheson, the faculty of taste's functioning is the last mental step in the experience of beauty. Such a faculty of taste's only contribution to the experience of beauty is the pleasure it produces. Kant conceives of the faculty of taste in a very different way, namely, as certain cognitive faculties—the understanding and the imagination—functioning in an unusual way. This conception places the faculty of taste in a "forward" position in the mind; that is, its functioning occurs at the very beginning of the mental process that underlies the experience of beauty. Consequently, for Kant, the faculty of taste is positioned to have an effect on the whole subsequent mental process underlying the experience of beauty. The character of our experience of objects with real existence is due, in part, according to Kant, to the ordinary functioning of the imagination and the understanding together with the functioning of the other cognitive faculties. An experience of the beautiful—whether of natural object or work of art—by contrast, results from the understanding and the imagination functioning in a nonordinary way that Kant calls "free play." The experience of the beautiful is thus cognitively different from ordinary experience because in it certain cognitive structures work differently. In ordinary experience, the cognitive faculties function to tie together and relate the appearances in the flow of awareness; that is, the forms of intuition assure a temporal and spatial synthesis and the understanding and the imagination assure a second synthesis (causal, substantial, and so forth) required for full-blown experience. Although Kant is very uninformative about what free play itself really is, in the way I am reading him, what the "free play" of the understanding and the imagination does is disconnect its object from the relations assured by the second synthesis, thereby experientially isolating it to a certain degree. For Kant, on this interpretation a beautiful object is experienced as devoid of certain relations, whereas an ordinary object is experienced as an intersection of a complete set of relations. A beautiful object is not an object in the full Kantian sense; it is to a degree a relationless object in the flow of experience. A beautiful object will of course have the spatial and temporal properties that are *internal* to it, just as an ordinary object would have. And a beautiful object will have spatial and temporal properties that relate it to other objects during the duration of an experience, but these properties will not be "filled in" in a causal or substantive way. Thus, a beautiful object will be—as compared to an ordinary object—a relationless object. Kant claims that a beautiful object is a form of purpose. What this means is that a beautiful object lacks the causal, substantive, and other characteristics that an object would have to have in order to be experienced as a functional or purposive thing. A beautiful object in order to be experienced at all would have to have some sort of duration through some period of time; it is unclear to me how this is accomplished on Kant's theory. (See Figure 3.)

Kant, like Burke, rejected Hutcheson's conception of the faculty of taste, and no doubt he did so because from the point of his "critical philosophy" there is no real evidence for the existence of such a mental structure. Of course, having a good reason for rejecting Hutcheson's conception is not a reason in favor of Kant's conception —that the faculty of taste is the imagination and the understanding in free play. Kant requires an *a priori* structure such as the Hutchesonian internal sense of beauty for his theory, but he has no way of justifying a conception like Hutcheson's. Kant was assured, however, of the existence of the imagination and the understanding because they are required as a basis of ordinary experience; he had them, so to speak, from *The Critique of Pure Reason*. In any event, what he does is to assert that the imagination and the understanding (*a priori* structures of the mind) are the faculty of taste when they function in a nonordinary way.

31

Ordinary experience

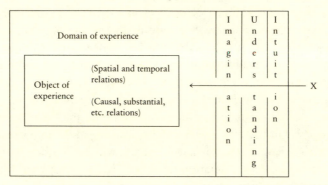

Experience of beauty

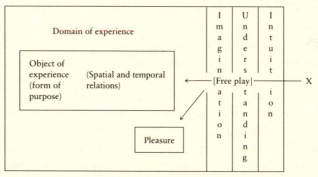

FIGURE 3

For Kant, in the cases of both ordinary experience and the experience of beauty, stimulation comes into the mind from the external world (X), and in both cases faculties of the mind (the forms of intuition, the imagination, and the understanding) structure that stimulation so as to constitute the objects of experience. In the experience of beauty, the imagination and the understanding function as the faculty of taste by engaging in "free play." The free play of these cognitive faculties constitutes the object of experience of beauty in such a way that it lacks certain relational features. The universal feature that Kant alleges the object of taste to have—the *form* of purpose—is derived from the forms of intuitions that function in the same way in both ordinary experience and the experience of beauty. Thus, the object of taste exhibits the *form* of purpose without actually exhibiting purpose (or function) because having a purpose (or function) would require the ordinary functioning of the imagination and the understanding.

The result of conceiving of the faculty of taste as the imagination and the understanding in free play, as I am understanding it, is that it becomes impossible for Kant to give an account of how the word "Napoleon" in *War and Peace* or any other reference to the actual world in a work of art can function to refer *when the work is experienced as an object of taste*. But, of course, such references occur and play an important role in our experience of many works of art.

Whatever the disadvantages of hypothesizing, as Hutcheson does, that the faculty of taste is reactive and comes into play only at the end of the mental process that underlies the experience of beauty, it does not have the disadvantage of nullifying the representational aspects of art when that art is an object of taste.

Thus, on this interpretation, Kant's conception of the faculty of taste is the historical source of the aesthetic-attitude movement that has so influenced the present-day conception of aesthetic experience as the proper experience of art. Kant, therefore, can be seen as largely responsible for the view—of the aesthetic-attitude theorists and some others—that the proper experience of art nullifies the referential aspects of art and makes their presence in art inexplicable.

The interpretation I have given of Kant's account of the experience of beauty might be called a constitutive one because according to it the imagination and the understanding constitute the experience of beauty and ordinary experience differently. It might be argued that for Kant the separation of beauty and interest is brought about by abstraction rather than by the constituting power of cognitive faculties. My reasons for advancing the constitutive interpretation is that this way of reading Kant provides a clear bridge to Schopenhauer's influential views, and it must have been the way in which Schopenhauer read Kant.

Schopenhauer's views are *almost* those of a full-blown aesthetic-attitude theorist. Whereas Kant retained all the trappings of the theory of taste—a faculty of taste (the imagination and the understanding in free play), a specific kind of object of taste (a form of purpose), and pleasure—Schopenhauer retains from Kant only the notion of cognitive faculties functioning in a nonordinary way.[12] He attached to this Kantian notion some Platonic and oriental metaphysics that would have horrified Kant. One result of these ontological importations is that Schopenhauer's view is not quite an aesthetic-attitude theory in the present-day sense because he maintains that aesthetic consciousness must have as its object some Platonic Idea and the present-day view holds that any object whatsoever can be an aesthetic object. Strictly speaking, Schopenhauer's view is neither fish nor fowl, but is a transition between the theory of taste and aesthetic-attitude theory. (One might read Schopenhauer's theory as an aesthetic-attitude view of a certain restricted kind, namely, as the view that aesthetic consciousness can take as its object any Platonic Idea whatsoever. Aesthetic consciousness cannot take any object whatsoever, but it can take any object whatsoever from a restricted domain, namely, Platonic Ideas.)

In any event, there is embedded in the vast, eclectic structure that is Schopenhauer's philosophy a conception that comes very close to being an aesthetic-attitude theory, and it was this conception that was subsequently so influential. Few, if any, were influenced by what Schopenhauer said about the place of Platonic Ideas in aesthetic experience, but many were influenced by his account of aesthetic consciousness.

What, then, is the nature of aesthetic or disinterested consciousness, according to Schopenhauer? The picture he gives of ordinary consciousness is of the intellect (the cognitive faculties) totally in the service of the will. In ordinary consciousness the objects of perception are simply the intersections of sets of temporal, spatial, and causal relations because it is through knowledge of these relations that the will is served. Aesthetic consciousness, by contrast, is very different and rare. The infrequent transition to aesthetic consciousness "can happen only by a change in the subject."[13] This change in the subject occurs when a person is "raised up by the power of the mind . . . [to] . . . relinquish the ordinary ways of considering things."[14] The change "takes place suddenly, . . . [when] . . . knowledge tears itself free from the service of the will."[15] When aesthetic consciousness is achieved, what before was perceived as the intersection of relations is then perceived as a perceptually relationless Platonic Idea. The Platonic Idea then becomes the object of aesthetic contemplation. Aesthetic consciousness is not only infrequent; it is precarious. Schopenhauer writes, "What makes this state difficult and therefore rare is that in it the . . . intellect . . . subdues and eliminates the . . . will, although only for a short time."[16] Furthermore, the aesthetic state can be maintained "only when we ourselves have no interest in . . . [the objects of perception; that is,] . . . they stand in no relation to our will."[17] "The absolute silence of the will . . . [is] required for the purely objective apprehension of the true nature of things [Platonic Ideas]."[18] Finally, the aesthetic "state is conditioned from the outside by our remaining wholly foreign to, and detached from, the scene to be contemplated, and not being at all actively involved in it."[19]

First, Schopenhauer's account of aesthetic consciousness does not involve any sort of noncognitive faculty of taste as does Hutcheson's theory of taste; the whole account is in terms of the intellect and its objects. Second, aesthetic consciousness depends on or is conditioned by the intellect's ability to act in such a way as to detach the object of its perception from its relations and make it perceptually relationless. Third, for Schopenhauer, once the detaching and isolating act occurs, disinterested contemplation of an object of perception becomes possible. Fourth, if any trace of the will manages to breach the isolating action of the intellect, aesthetic consciousness is destroyed; there is an absolute antagonism between aesthetic consciousness and interest.

How, on Schopenhauer's view, does artistic imitation or representation work into his conception of aesthetic experience?

Consider a portrait of Napoleon. A Schopenhauerian aesthetic experience of the portrait would be an experience of a detached and relationless object, such that the relation of the portrait to Napoleon is obliterated. A proper experience of the portrait, as envisaged by Schopenhauer, has no role for ordinary representation, that is, the representation of things in the empirical world. In a proper experience of the work, the object of the experience would be a Platonic Idea—presumably the Platonic Idea of Man. Insofar as representation occurs in a proper experience of such a work of art, it is what might be called "super-representation," that is, representation of a Platonic Idea.

Schopenhauer rejects ordinary imitation in favor of super-imitation. The inheritors of the Schopenhauerian tradition had no interest in super-imitation and its entailed ontology, but they perpetuated his rejection of ordinary imitation.

Disinterestedness has meant different things in different theories. For Shaftesbury, disinterestedness means that the experience of a beautiful object is not motivated by selfishness or as such involved in any way with an anticipated benefit; the experience of a beautiful object is just an experience of that object independent of whatever relations it has to other things (including future mental states of the person who is having the experience). For Shaftesbury, whatever relation a beautiful object has to another thing is just irrelevant to its beauty. Hutcheson and the earlier theorists of taste agreed with Shaftesbury and devoted their energies to developing theories of mental structures that would explain why the experience of a beautiful object is as Shaftesbury says it is. Kant's theory of the faculty of taste as I have interpreted it introduces a crucial change. For Kant, the experience of a beautiful object is not just an experience of that object separable from whatever relations it has to other things; it is an experience of that object in which whatever relations it has to other things have been experientially nullified. Schopenhauer and his followers have perpetuated this Kantian doctrine, which eliminates from the experience of beauty not only desire of future benefit but imitation and any other relation the object of beauty has to anything outside the experience. This Kantian-Schopenhauerian doctrine of the nature of what the experience of art ought to be is very different from our actual experiences of art and has, consequently, distorted our conception of what the nature of art experiences ought to be.

CHAPTER THREE

The Artistically Good: Ziff

A new era for the theory of art evaluation began in 1958 with the publication of Paul Ziff's "Reasons in Art Criticism"[1] and Chapters X and XI of Monroe Beardsley's *Aesthetics: Problems in the Philosophy of Criticism*.[2] Each philosopher presents an ingenious instrumentalist theory with little or no attention paid to the metalinguistic questions that so concerned other philosophers of the time. Both theories have to some extent incorporated the anti-cognitivism of the Schopenhauerian tradition, although this aspect is more explicit and obvious in Beardsley's theory, because his theory is worked out at greater length and in greater detail. I shall, consequently, focus more on the anti-cognitivism of Beardsley's theory and say little about this deficiency in Ziff's account. I shall consider Paul Ziff's theory first, and discuss Beardsley's more developed view in the next chapter.

Ziff's article, although written in a difficult style, remains one of the few truly stimulating pieces by present-day philosophers on the theory of art evaluation. There are, however, several technical difficulties with the way in which Ziff formulates the basic principle of his theory. I shall propose ways to remedy these difficulties and thereby strengthen Ziff's theory. When I have completed these repairs, I shall inquire briefly into the adequacy and completeness of his theory.

At the end of his article as a sort of summary, Ziff formulates a definition of "good work of art" in terms of necessary and sufficient conditions. I rewrite his definition completely in English and without the symbolic abbreviation he uses as follows:

1. A work of art is good if and only if the performance of the relevant action on that work by a particular person under appropriate conditions is worthwhile for its own sake.[3]

There are, for Ziff, three things involved in the worthwhileness of the experience that underlies the evaluation of a work of art: appropriate conditions, a relevant action, and a particular person performing the relevant action.

First, how does one know what the appropriate conditions are? Ziff's answer is that a particular work of art determines the conditions under which it is to be experienced. If one understands a particular work of art, then one will know the conditions that are appropriate for experiencing it.

Second, how does one know if a particular action is the relevant one? Ziff's answer is that the particular work of art determines the relevant action. Again, if one understands a particular work of art, then one will know which action is relevant for it. One painting requires the action of contemplation, another painting requires the action of scanning, another the action of studying, another the action of observing, another the action of surveying, or inspecting or examining or scrutinizing and so on. He classifies contemplation, scanning, studying, and the like under the general heading of acts of *aspection*. Ziff claims that there are hundreds of different acts of aspection, any one of which may be relevant to a particular painting. We discover which actions are relevant, he says, "by trial and error. The relevant actions are those that prove worthwhile in connection with the particular work"[4] His use of the notion of aspection, the act of viewing, to characterize the proper experience of a work of art is, I think, indicative of his anti-cognitivism. That the proper experience of a work of art is a matter of the proper kind of viewing suggests, although it does not prove, that the seeing of the "surfaces" of works of art is the only important thing and that understanding a work's cognitive relations has no role to play in a work's value. This view of the proper experience of works of art shows, I believe, the influence of the Schopenhauerian tradition on Ziff. There is, however, one passage concerning subject matter in Ziff's article in which he seems to attribute importance to works' cognitive relations. He writes:

> A painting with a trivial subject, a shoe, a cabbage, may be a superb work, but its range is limited: even if it succeeds, it is not great, not sublime; and if it fails, its failure is of no consequence. . . . But a figure painting, Signorelli's Pan, was a great, a sublime painting; had it failed, its failure would have been more tragic than trivial.[5]

In this passage and the one that follows it, Ziff seems to be saying that a work's subject matter is significant but that its significance relates not to the work's goodness but to some further value dimension. Unfortunately, he does not develop this point; so it is not clear how far or if Ziff deviates from the Schopenhauerian tradition.

Third, how does one know if a particular person is adequate to perform the relevant action? Ziff's answer is, I believe, that a particular person is adequate if he or she is able to perform the relevant action under appropriate conditions.

Ziff's evaluation scheme can be diagrammed in Figure 4. Ziff's conception of dependency relations between works of art, conditions, actions, and persons is an interesting idea, and it is necessary to have it in mind in order to understand Ziff's theory. In any event,

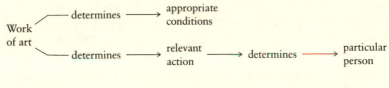

FIGURE 4

however significant Ziff's idea is, I shall pursue it only briefly at the end of this chapter. In this chapter, I shall focus primarily on the value terminology of the definition.

William Kennick, in his anthology,[6] has raised a question about Ziff's definition that can be formulated in the following way. The biconditional definition logically implies a conditional statement of sufficiency:

2. If the performance of the relevant action on a work of art by a particular person under appropriate conditions is worthwhile for its own sake, then that work is good.

If it is assumed as a hypothesis that

3. The performance of the relevant action on that work by Josef under appropriate conditions is worthwhile for its own sake.

It follows from 2 and 3 that

4. The work of art is good.

The biconditional definition also logically implies a conditional statement of necessity:

5. If a work of art is good, then the performance of the relevant action on that work by a particular person under appropriate conditions is worthwhile for its own sake.

If it is assumed as a hypothesis that

> 6. The performance of the relevant action on that work by George under appropriate conditions is *not* worthwhile for its own sake.

It follows from 5 and 6 that

> 7. The work of art is *not* good.

And if 4 and 7 are combined, we get the contradiction:

> 8. The work of art is good and *not* good.

Kennick, having produced the contradiction, does not speculate about how Ziff might respond to this criticism.

One way for Ziff to avoid the contradiction would be to argue that if one person performed *the* relevant action on a work under appropriate conditions and found it worthwhile, then it would be impossible for anyone else to perform the same relevant action on the same work under the same appropriate conditions and not find it worthwhile. Thus, the hypothesis formulated as 6 is impossible and the contradiction cannot arise. It is not clear to me that Ziff can make this argument; at least, there is nothing in "Reasons in Art Criticism" that enables him to do so.

Another way to avoid the contradiction would be to reformulate Ziff's definition by substituting "can be worthwhile" for "is worthwhile."

> 1*a*. A work of art is good if and only if the performance of the relevant action on that work by a particular person under appropriate conditions *can be* worthwhile for its own sake.

This formulation resembles Beardsley's definition of "good aesthetic object," which will be quoted later in this chapter, in that both are formulated in capacity terms. The necessity condition derivable from the new formulation of Ziff's definition would then also be stated in terms of capacity and would read:

5*a*. If a work of art is good, then the performance of the relevant action on that work by a particular person under appropriate conditions *can be* worthwhile for its own sake.

The capacity version of the necessity condition eliminates the problem raised for Ziff's formulation by George's not finding the work worthwhile. The fact that George does not find the work worthwhile together with the capacity version of the necessity condition does not entail that the work is not good. This is clearly shown if 5*a* and 6 are placed together as premises of an argument.

5*a*. If a work of art is good, then the performance of the relevant action on that work by a particular person under appropriate conditions *can be* worthwhile for its own sake.

6. The performance of the relevant action on that work by George under appropriate conditions *is not* worthwhile for its own sake.

The two premises just do not fit together in a way that licenses any inference. Thus, no contradiction arises from Josef's and George's having differing experiences.

The capacity formulation of the definition has the effect of virtually neutralizing the necessity condition part of the definition. If the work is good, it just states the obvious that someone's action can be worthwhile. On the other hand, anyone's not finding the action worthwhile just fails to mesh with the necessity condition. The only set of conditions that can mesh with the necessity condition is that in which no one could find the relevant action worthwhile. It will be very difficult to show that this universal negative situation is the case. In effect, the sufficiency condition part of the definition assumes great importance and it can be reformulated as follows:

2. If the performance of the relevant action on a work of art by a particular person under appropriate conditions *can be* worthwhile for its own sake, then that work is good.

If the performance of the relevant action on a given work by Josef under appropriate conditions is worthwhile for its own sake, then that work of art is good. Furthermore, Josef's or anyone else's finding the relevant action worthwhile shows that the universal negative situation required to trigger the necessity condition for a given work does not obtain.

The theory, considered essentially as the sufficiency condition, is not without technical problems. As Ziff formulates the sufficiency condition, it is too strong (if one looks at the consequence) or too weak (if one looks at the antecedent). What I mean is this: both the antecedent and the consequence of this sufficiency conditional contain value terms: "worthwhile" and "good." The value of the work of art is determined by the value, that is, the worthwhileness, of a person's experience. Ziff's evaluational theory is an instrumentalist one, and his theory, that is, the sufficiency conditional, can be represented in Figure 5. If when someone interacts with a work of art

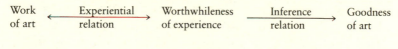

FIGURE 5

it produces a worthwhile experience, then it can be inferred that the work is a good one. I find no difficulty with instrumentalism as such. The difficulty I do find results from the fact that worthwhileness of experience admits of degrees or something like degrees and may be described in the following ways:

45

"the experience was totally worthwhile,"
"the experience was well worthwhile,"
"the experience was worthwhile,"
"the experience was worthwhile—so so,"
"the experience was barely worthwhile," and the like.

Although it seems reasonable that an experience that is at the high end of the worthwhileness order justifies the conclusion that a work of art is good or better than good, an experience that is at the bottom of the worthwhileness scale can scarcely justify the conclusion that a work of art is good.

Ziff's instrumentalism and the difficulty of his particular formulation can be understood in the following way: The properties of a work of art can be the object of an experience that is worthwhile in some degree, and on the basis of the worthwhileness of the experience, the goodness or value of the work can be *inferred*. The problem with Ziff's view can be made clear in the following way. Consider a scale for the measurement of the worthwhileness of experience that runs from zero to one. This scale is construed either to run continuously from zero to the maximum degree of worthwhileness or to run from zero to one with a relatively small number of discrete positions corresponding to *barely worthwhile, well worthwhile,* and the like on up to the maximum of worthwhileness. The worthwhileness scale is either a continuous scale of degrees or a discrete scale, that is, either $0 \rule{1.5cm}{0.4pt} 1$ or $0 \times \times \times 1$. (I am not sure which is the best or the correct way to construe the scale. Assume for present purposes that it is discrete.) Consider a second scale for the measurement of the *goodness* or *value* of works of art that runs from zero to one and on which there is a threshold point above which a work of art is *at least good*. The goodness or value scale would be $0 \rule{1cm}{0.4pt} * \rule{0.8cm}{0.4pt} 1$. At the threshold point and to its right lie the value measurements of *good, excellent, magnificent,* and the like. Below the threshold point and to its left lie the value measures of *mediocre, poor, bad,* and the like. (I ignore here the question of whether the value scale is one of continuous degree or is discrete.) Ziff's sufficiency conditional can be fully represented in Figure 6. As

Work of art ←—— Experiential relation ——→ O X X X I (Worthwhileness of experience) ——— Inference relation ——→ O____*___I (Goodness of art)

FIGURE 6

it stands, Ziff's statement of sufficiency fails to say anything about how high the measure on the worthwhileness of experience scale (in the middle of the diagram) must be in order to license an inference to the threshold point or above on the goodness of art scale (on the right in the diagram). If it is known simply that a work generates an experience that is worthwhile, the only thing that could follow about the work is that it has goodness or value of some degree or other, which is a much weaker conclusion than that it is good. Ziff's theory requires supplementation that coordinates the positions on the two scales.

Consider for comparison Monroe Beardsley's formulation of the central definition of his instrumentalist evaluational theory.

"X is a *good* aesthetic object" means "X is capable of producing *good* aesthetic experiences (that is, aesthetic experiences of a fairly great magnitude)."[7]

(Beardsley's definition, as noted earlier, is formulated in a capacity way, so the problem of contradiction raised for Ziff by Josef's and George's having different value experiences does not arise for Beardsley, but this is not the question with which I am concerned at the moment. I realize, by the way, that Beardsley is defining "good aesthetic object" whereas Ziff is defining "good work of art" and that *aesthetic object* and *work of art* are different notions, but this difference is not significant for the present point.)

47

Notice that for Beardsley, as for Ziff, value terms occur on both sides of the definition. Beardsley, however, balances the value terms on the two sides. "*Good* aesthetic object" in the defined part of the definition is *balanced* by "*good* aesthetic experiences" in the defining part of the definition. Beardsley also specifies that a good aesthetic experience is one of fairly great magnitude. Thus, in the sufficiency conditional derivable from Beardsley's definition, there is no imbalance of value terms. Beardsley's sufficiency conditional would read as follows:

> If X is capable of producing *good* aesthetic experiences (that is, aesthetic experiences of a fairly great magnitude), then X is a *good* aesthetic object.

There are difficulties with Beardsley's theory, as will be shown, but it does not suffer from the kind of imbalance that Ziff's theory does.

With the distinctions about worthwhileness of experience in mind, Ziff's definition of "good work of art" can be formulated in a balanced way as well as in a way that avoids contradiction.

> 1c. A work of art is *good* if and only if the performance of the relevant action on that work by a particular person under appropriate conditions can be *well* worthwhile for its own sake.

Ziff's sufficiency condition will now read as follows:

> 2a. If the performance of the relevant action on a work by a particular person under appropriate conditions can be *well* worthwhile for its own sake, then that work is *good*.

Having raised and in a formal way resolved the balance problem in Ziff's theory, I want now to note several things about his

48

view. First, Ziff's biconditional and the derivable necessity and suf-ficiency conditionals in either their original or reformulated versions function as *principles* for criticism. These principles together with premises that mesh with them would enable one to draw value con-clusions about particular works of art. For example, the sufficiency conditional and a meshing premise function as follows.

If the performance of the relevant action of contemplation on this work by a particular person under appropriate conditions can be well worthwhile for its own sake, then this work of art is good.

The performance of the relevant action of contemplation on this work by Josef under appropriate conditions is well worthwhile for its own sake.

Therefore, this work of art is good.

Notice that this is a finished (and deductively valid) argument, but that it does not contain any reference to a reason—the presumed topic of Ziff's "Reasons in Art Criticism." At the very end of his arti-cle, however, Ziff does discuss the place of reasons in art criticism. He defines a reason as follows: "A reason why a work of art is good is a fact about the work in virtue of which the performance of a relevant action by a particular person under appropriate conditions is worthwhile for its own sake."[8] Ziff adds, "Reasons in criticism are worthwhile because they tell us what to do with the work, and that is worth knowing."[9] Thus, for Ziff, reasons have a very impor-tant *informal* role to play in criticism, but they do not appear in the formal argument whose conclusion is an evaluation of a work of art.

If Ziff's reformulated theory is right, it is possible to draw con-clusions about the specific values of works of art. On this basis, it seems that one ought then to be able to make value comparisons among works of art: a good work is better than a not good work, two good works are of approximately the same value, and so on.

But if one reflects on what underlies the value judgments of works of art, it is not so clear that comparisons can always really be made. Consider the comparison of two good works: one work may be good because *contemplating* it is well worthwhile but another work may be good because *scanning* it is well worthwhile. On the surface, both are good and thus seemingly comparable, but on a deeper level the actions that are the basis for these evaluations are different actions. Are well-worthwhile contemplations and well-worthwhile scannings of approximately the same value? We seem to have an apples-and-oranges comparison. In making this remark I do not mean to suggest that this "difficulty" with comparisons is a fault in Ziff's theory. I just wish to note that his view does not satisfy the traditional philosophical craving for comparing works of art. Indeed, as I shall try to show in the final chapter, the traditional craving cannot be completely satisfied.

The final point I want to make about Ziff's theory involves his attempt to deal with the problem of relativism. The capacity formulation of Ziff's biconditional and its sufficiency condition has the effect of making the mentioning of particular persons in the formulation of the definition or the sufficiency conditional of "good work of art" seemingly unnecessary. In any event, Ziff appears to think that persons need not be mentioned, as is shown by the exasperated remark he makes after a discussion of what is required of a person qualified to test the value of art. "There is no point in worrying about persons for practically nothing can be done about them. Actions are what matter." [10] In order to represent Ziff's declared view, Figure 4 can be simplified by eliminating the reference to particular persons (see Figure 7). A person is, of course, required to experience a work of art for an evaluation to be made, but it is simply a person who can perform the relevant action. Ziff's attempt to eliminate persons from the picture is an attempt at avoiding relativism. If actions are the important thing and only one action is relevant to a given work of art, then it appears that relativism can be avoided. But Ziff does

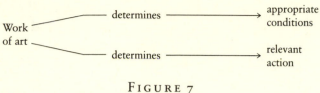

FIGURE 7

not show that it is impossible for two persons to perform the same action on the same work and one of them find it worthwhile and the other find it not worthwhile. The reformulated capacity version of Ziff's definition of "good work of art" does not help in this regard. The new version avoids the problem of contradiction and, hence, relativism at the level of statements about works of art when two persons disagree over the worthwhileness of the experience of a work of art, but it does not avoid relativism at the level of the worthwhileness of the experience when people disagree over the worthwhileness of the experience of a particular work of art. That is, Ziff's reformulated theory avoids the relativism of a fully qualified Josef's concluding that a particular work of art is good and a fully qualified George's concluding that the same work is not good, but the theory does not avoid a fully qualified Josef's finding the experience of that particular work worthwhile and a fully qualified George's finding the experience of the same work not worthwhile. Ziff's conception of a particular kind of action as the experience that tests the value of a work of art is a thought-provoking one, but it is not one that is sufficiently developed for us to see if it can really solve the problem of relativism at the level of the worthwhileness of experience.

I turn now to the consideration of Monroe Beardsley's theory of art evaluation, the most completely developed theory formulated thus far by any philosopher.

CHAPTER FOUR

A Theory of Art Evaluation: Beardsley

As noted at the beginning of the last chapter, Monroe Beardsley first proposed his theory of art evaluation in 1958 in his book *Aesthetics: Problems in the Philosophy of Criticism*.[1] His theory, which is worked out in great detail, is a substantive, nonmetalinguistic theory. Like Ziff's, Beardsley's theory is an instrumentalist one. Beardsley, however, unlike Ziff, proposes that art is to be evaluated on the basis of how well it can produce aesthetic experience—aesthetic experience being valuable. Since Beardsley initially proposed his theory, he has periodically repaired and refined it, but certain central features of the theory have remained unchanged. Although it cannot be said that his view is an aesthetic-attitude one, throughout the various changes it has undergone Beardsley's theory of aesthetic experience has retained the Schopenhauerian feature of detachedness. For Beardsley, the aesthetic object at the center of aesthetic experience is conceived of as an experientially relationless object.

I shall divide my exposition of Beardsley's theory into four sections, beginning with a section on his account of aesthetic experience —the foundation of his theory. In the three sections that follow, I shall develop various of the technical details of his theory. My exposition will not only give an account of Beardsley's theory as he developed it, but will try to bring out features of the theory that are implicit and of which Beardsley was unaware. (By the way, I think it is almost always true that philosophers are unaware of some of the implications of their theories, so it is not surprising that Beardsley is.) In the fifth and final section I shall try to undermine Beardsley's notion of aesthetic experience as the foundation of art criticism. Although I believe his theory in the final analysis is defective, it is nevertheless a wonderfully ingenious and useful theory and well worth the considerable space that I shall devote to it. Beardsley, in working out his theory, identifies and illustrates all of the features that a theory of art evaluation must have; no one else has come close to doing this. In short, Beardsley's theory of art evaluation is an achievement of the first order.

I. THE THEORY OF AESTHETIC EXPERIENCE

At an early point in his discussion of critical reasons in his book and long before he outlines his view of aesthetic experience, Beardsley raises the question of the relevance of cognitive and moral aspects of works of art for evaluation. Without argument, he says that cognitive and moral reasons can be "set aside as not of concern here." He says at this point that he is concerned only with "reasons that are peculiarly aesthetic."[2] It is not until much later in his book when he has developed his theory of aesthetic experience that one can see why he thinks he is free to set aside cognitive and moral aspects of works of art as irrelevant to the evaluation of art.

I begin by examining in considerable detail Beardsley's conception of aesthetic experience, because it is the foundation of his theory. I shall first outline the account of aesthetic experience he gave in 1958 in his book. After that, I shall move directly to the account of aesthetic experience that he presented in his presidential address to the Eastern Division of the American Philosophical Association in

1978, ignoring the various modifications of his view he attempted between these two accounts.[3]

In the earlier account of 1958, Beardsley outlines the, presumably essential, features of aesthetic experience.

1. In aesthetic experience, attention is firmly fixed on a perceptual object that controls the experience.

2. The experience has an intensity that concentrates our attention narrowly.

3. Elements of the experience cohere with one another.

4. Elements of the experience complete one another.

5. The experience will be of some complexity or other.

The intensity, unity (coherence and completeness), and complexity referred to are what Beardsley calls "phenomenally subjective features" of aesthetic experience and are distinct from the perceived intensity, unity, and complexity of works of art, which Beardsley calls "phenomenally objective features" of works of art in aesthetic experience. The kinds of things that Beardsley has in mind when he talks about the phenomenally objective unity, complexity, and intensity of works of art are as follows. The phenomenally objective unity of a painting, for example, might result from the repeated occurrence of a similar shape or from the use of harmonizing colors. The phenomenally objective complexity of a painting is simply the function of the number of elements that can be visually discriminated. For example, a painting that is uniformly one color is less complex than a painting that is uniformly one color except that it has a dot of contrasting color. The phenomenally objective intensity of a painting might result, for example, from the use of two strongly contrasting colors. The phenomenally objective intensity, unity, and complexity of works of art are causally related to (that is, are the cause of) the phenomenally subjective intensity, unity, and complexity of aesthetic experience. Thus, aesthetic experience contains the phenomenally objective intensity, unity, and complexity of the work of art and the phenomenally subjective intensity, unity, and complexity of aesthetic experience. According to Beardsley's theory, there is in aesthetic experience a kind of mirroring and doubling of characteristics.

The sixth characteristic of aesthetic experience, as Beardsley conceives of it, is its detached or disinterested nature. The detachedness of the experience supposedly derives from two sources: (1) it arises as a consequence of some of the other characteristics of aesthetic experience and (2) it arises as a consequence of the nature of works of art. The detached nature is, therefore, a second-order characteristic. The first-order characteristics of fixed attention, intensity, coherence, and completeness work together to produce detachedness. Firmly fixed attention isolates the experience from its background. The intensity (concentratedness) of the experience shuts out distractions and irrelevant thoughts. The coherence of the experience excludes things that do not fit in. Because of its completeness, the "experience detaches itself, and even insulates itself, from the intrusion of alien elements."[4] The detached nature of the experience, as noted, also has origins in the nature of works of art or, as Beardsley says, "aesthetic objects." "There is something lacking in [aesthetic objects] . . . that keeps them from being quite real, from achieving the full status of things—or, better, that prevents the question of reality from arising. They are complexes of qualities, surfaces."[5] The unreality of works of art in part causes the experience of them to have an unreal or detached quality. The detached nature means that the experience itself has, as Beardsley says, "no practical purpose" and is "without any necessary commitment to practical action."[6]

In his 1978 account of aesthetic experience, it is still the notions of subjective intensity, unity, and complexity that are the primary focus of his attention although they are not referred to as explicitly as in the earlier account. The notions of objective intensity, unity, and complexity are still held to function as before by Beardsley. In this later account, Beardsley cites five "symptoms" of aesthetic experience, of which only the first is essential. This essential feature, called "object-directedness," is virtually identical with the first feature of the earlier account. Of the remaining four "symptoms," only three (any three) of them are required by Beardsley for an aesthetic experience. The five symptoms are as follows:

1. A willingly accepted guidance over the succession of one's mental states by phenomenally objective properties (qualities and relations) of a perceptual or intentional field on which attention is fixed with a feeling that things are working or have worked themselves out fittingly. Since this awareness is directed by, as well as to, the object, we may call this feature, for short, *object-directedness*.

2. A sense of actively exercising constructive powers of mind, of being challenged by a variety of potentially conflicting stimuli to try to make them cohere; a keyed-up state amounting to exhilaration in seeing connections between percepts and meanings, a sense (which may be illusory) of achieved intelligibility. For short: *active discovery*.

3. A sense of integration as a person, of being restored to wholeness from distracting and disruptive impulses (but by inclusive synthesis as well as by exclusion), and a corresponding contentment, even through disturbing feelings, that involve self-acceptance and self-expansion. For short: *a sense of wholeness*.

4. A sense of freedom, of release from the dominance of some antecedent concerns about past and future, a relaxation and sense of harmony with what is presented or semantically involved by it or implicitly promised by it, so that what comes has the air of having been freely chosen. For short: *felt freedom*.

5. A sense that the objects on which interest is concentrated are set a little at a distance emotionally—a certain detachment of affect so that even when we are confronted with dark and terrible things, and feel them sharply, they do not oppress but make us aware of our power to rise above them. For short: *detached affect.*[7]

It may now appear that Beardsley does not require detachedness as an essential feature of aesthetic experience because *detached affect* is one of four characteristics of which only three are required. *Felt freedom,* however, is another way of characterizing detachedness, and either *felt freedom* or *detached affect* is necessary on Beardsley's view. In fact, *felt freedom* and *detached affect* seem more like two aspects of one complex feature than two distinct ones. Each of the two alleged distinct features speaks of the nonpractical and insular nature of aesthetic experience. What the two seem to be saying is that aesthetic experience is detached from concerns of past, present, and future, that is, cut off in a decisive way from the remainder of experience. Independent of the criteria that Beardsley lists here, the dispute he was having with Goodman over reference as an element of aesthetic experience at about the same time he was writing his presidential address is further evidence that he regards aesthetic experience as detached; otherwise he would have been able to accept some of Goodman's points.[8]

In his presidential address, Beardsley does not repeat his remark about the unreality of aesthetic objects, that is, works of art, but he does give a characterization of works of art that relates them necessarily to aesthetic experience. He writes, "So an artwork can be usefully defined as an intentional arrangement of conditions for affording experiences with marked aesthetic character."[9] Presumably, he also still thinks that works of art are in some sense unreal and that this feature contributes to the detachedness of aesthetic experience.

It is a deeply entrenched view of conventional philosophical wisdom that aesthetic experience is detached or disinterested, and Beardsley's theory is but one of the most recent expressions of that view. The notion that aesthetic experience is disinterested or detached and that the object of aesthetic experience is experientially relationless had become a commonplace of twentieth-century aesthetic-attitude theories. The aesthetic-attitude theorists, following Schopenhauer, claimed that there is aesthetic perception, aesthetic attention, or something of the sort, that is, a cognitive mental function that is responsible for producing disinterested or detached units of experience. Beardsley has inherited the view that aesthetic experience is disinterested from these followers of Schopenhauer but with an important difference. In earlier views a special mental function—aesthetic consciousness, aesthetic perception, aesthetic attention—is cited as the reason why the content of aesthetic experience is disinterested or detached. There is no such theoretical element in Beardsley's view; so he must explain the detached nature of aesthetic experience in some other way. The only serious alternative way of justifying the disinterestedness of aesthetic experience is as the conclusion of an inductive survey of examples of experiences of art. I will examine this kind of justification in the concluding section of this chapter.

At this point, it will be useful to try to give an account of the aesthetic experience of a work of art as Beardsley conceives of it. In addition to the subject who has the experience, there is the object of the experience, a work of art; the subject perceives the object. All of the aesthetically relevant features of the work are subsumed under one of three standard features of the object: unity, intensity, or complexity. The three features can be called "standard" because every object will have each of them to some degree or other. These three features can be called "aesthetically relevant" because only they, according to Beardsley, are always good-making characteristics of works of art. For any feature to make a contribution to the goodness of a work of art, it must either be one of the standard features (for example, be some degree of unity) or be something that contributes to one of the standard features (for example, be something that helps make for some degree of intensity). We might call these two kinds of features "standard" and "contributory." Any element of an aesthetic experience that is not either standard or contributory is irrelevant for determining the goodness of a work of art. For example, any moral value a work has is irrelevant to, as Beardsley puts it, the goodness of a work of art as art. The phrase "art as art" seems to distinguish for him those aspects of a work that contribute to aesthetic experience from those that do not. On Beardsley's view, the moral value of a work does not contribute to aesthetic experience. He does not say that works of art do not have moral or cognitive value, nor does he say that moral or cognitive value is unimportant. In fact, he thinks such value is significant but not to the value of art as art, that is, not significant to its capacity to produce aesthetic experience. The capacity of art to produce aesthetic experience is limited to its standard features.

Why this limitation? The limitation derives from the alleged insular nature of aesthetic experience. The unity, intensity, and complexity of a work of art are the kinds of things that can produce an experience that is detached from past, present, or future experiences. Moral and cognitive features of a work of art make no contribution to aesthetic experience. Furthermore, these two kinds of features stand in relation to things outside the aesthetic experience and, consequently, attention to them threatens the integrity of the aesthetic experience, that is, threatens to dissolve the experience by relating it to things outside of it. Moral and cognitive features of art are not only irrelevant to the evaluation of art as art, on Beardsley's view; they pose a threat to aesthetic experience.

II. INSTRUMENTAL INFERENCE

Aesthetic experience, as Beardsley conceives of it, is the foundation for the critical evaluation of art. I turn now to his account of the nature of critical argument—its principles, reasons, and conclusions, and its relation to aesthetic experience.

At this point, it will be useful to have a diagram of Beardsley's account of aesthetic experience and its relation to art (Figure 8).

Aesthetic experience

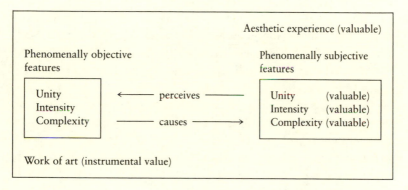

FIGURE 8

Beardsley's theory is a causal one in which the value of works of art derives from the ability of certain phenomenally objective features of works of art to produce valuable subjective features of experience—subjective unity, intensity, and complexity. (Beardsley also claims that there can be additional value that can result from an interaction between the objective and the subjective features of experience, but I shall ignore this complication.)

Beardsley's theory of the logic of art criticism—his account of principles and reasons—derives from and depends on his instrumentalist view of the value of art. I shall work out in some detail Beardsley's theory of principles and reasons, but in so doing, I shall not simply be summarizing what Beardsley has said because he did not fully see the implications of his own theory and, consequently, left certain parts of the theory undeveloped.

In his earliest discussion of the matter—in *Aesthetics: Problems in the Philosophy of Criticism*—Beardsley begins by taking the general form of critical evaluation to be of the form:

This work of art is good,   (the evaluation)

Because it has such and such a property.   (the reason)[10]

He then goes on to claim that some reasons involve generality. For example, if the reason given is "This work of art is unified," this implies that there is a general principle such as "Disunity is always a defect in works of art" or "Unity is a good-making feature of works of art."

Also, at this initial stage, Beardsley raises the question of whether critical arguments are deductive or inductive. His first conclusion is that inferences to "This work of art is good" cannot be deductive because a false general principle would be required to make the argument valid. The following kind of argument would, Beardsley thinks, be required:

All highly unified works of art are good.

This work of art is highly unified.

Therefore, this work of art is good.

Beardsley first claims (quite rightly) that the general principle in this argument is false. He further claims (wrongly) that, consequently, critical evaluation arguments cannot be deductive. Having drawn the conclusion that such arguments cannot be deductive, it would seem then that inferences to such conclusions as "This work of art is good" must be inductive, and Beardsley strongly suggests that they are.[11] He does not, however, explicitly draw the conclusion that such inferences are inductive and says that he will not be able to settle this issue until certain other questions are answered. I do not believe, however, that Beardsley ever returns to the question of the nature of this kind of inference in an explicit and theoretical way in *Aesthetics* or in any subsequent book or essay. Nor does he ever subsequently illustrate his apparent view that critical arguments are inductive in character by constructing a sample argument.

Perhaps the first thing to notice is that, although Beardsley asserts that a principle such as "All highly unified works of art are good" is false, he asserts that weaker principles such as "Unity is a good-making feature of works of art" are acceptable. This weaker principle may be restated equivalently as "A unified work always has some value." "Has some value" is a very weak predicate and is true of works from magnificent ones to those of the least possible value. By contrast, "is good" is a strong predicate with a narrower focus and is true only of works that exceed a certain threshold of value. With the weaker principle as a premise, the following valid *deductive* argument can be constructed:

A unified work of art always has some value.

This work of art is unified.

Therefore, this work of art has some value.

So, using Beardsley's own principle, a deductive critical argument can be constructed, although its conclusion is much weaker than the conclusion of the argument Beardsley used in making his argument that critical arguments are not deductive. He has in mind as the conclusion of an evaluative argument the strong "This work of art *is good,*" but the conclusions of evaluative arguments may have predicates that range from "has some value" through "is bad," "is mediocre," "is good," and "is magnificent."

Beardsley concludes that there are three general evaluational principles:

1. Unity is a good-making feature of works of art.

2. Intensity is a good-making feature of works of art.

3. Complexity is a good-making feature of works of art.

The relation of these three principles to Beardsley's conception of the aesthetic experience of art is clear: the subject term in each principle refers to one of the three phenomenally objective features in which Beardsley is so interested.

It is also clear at this point that even the statement that a work of art is unified, intense, and complex, together with the three principles, will not deductively yield the conclusion that a work of art is good but only that it has some value. Having all the good-making features cannot deductively ensure that a work is good. Even having each of the good-making features to a high degree cannot deductively ensure that a work is good.

The real moral of the story thus far is that an evaluative conclusion as strong as "This work of art is good" requires as a premise a strong principle—a principle stronger than any principle that Beardsley has in hand. I think that Beardsley's instrumentalist theory of value involves strong principles that can serve as strong premises, although Beardsley does not seem to have been aware of them or at least does not make any explicit use of them.

The very first step in the development of Beardsley's theory of value is his maintaining that works of art (he says, "aesthetic objects") have a function, namely, to induce aesthetic experiences. Given this step, he gives the following definition of "good aesthetic object":

"X is a good aesthetic object" means "X is capable of producing good aesthetic experiences (that is, aesthetic experiences of a fairly great magnitude)." [12]

He then says,

> I propose to say, simply, that "being a good aesthetic object" and "having aesthetic value" mean the same thing.

Given this equation, he gives the following definition:

> "X has aesthetic value" means "X has the capacity to produce an aesthetic experience of fairly great magnitude (such an experience having value)." [13]

The equation of "good aesthetic object" and "having aesthetic value" is a misstep. To say that something has aesthetic value is to say something quite broad: it covers cases from the smallest possible value to the greatest possible value. To say of something that it is a good aesthetic object is to say something more narrowly focused: it covers cases that surpass a threshold, cases that have enough value to be good. In the remainder of the discussion in his book, Beardsley uses the expression "aesthetic value," but I think he uses it to mean what is meant by the expression "aesthetically good." Beardsley's failing to note the difference in meaning of these two expressions may be to some extent responsible for his failing to see the possibility of his theory underwriting deductive critical evaluation arguments.

Recall now Beardsley's definition of "good aesthetic object":

> "X is a good aesthetic object" means "X is capable of producing good aesthetic experiences (that is, aesthetic experiences of a fairly great magnitude)."

The defining or "right-hand side" of the definition speaks explicitly of good aesthetic experiences and asserts that good aesthetic experiences are to be equated with aesthetic experiences of a fairly great magnitude. This is equivalent to claiming that the following generalization is true:

1. Aesthetic experiences of a fairly great magnitude are always good.

The definition of "good aesthetic object" also yields the following conditional, in which I substitute "work of art" for "aesthetic object" in order to limit the discussion to art.

2. If a work of art is capable of producing a good aesthetic experience, then the work of art is (instrumentally) good.

This second statement is a version of the definition of "instrumentally good" and, hence, does not depend simply on Beardsley's definition of "good aesthetic object." Now if in a given case we have the premise:

3. This work of art can produce an aesthetic experience of fairly great magnitude.

From 1 and 3 we can get

4. This work of art can produce a good aesthetic experience.

From 2 and 4 we can get

5. This work of art is (instrumentally) good.

All the steps in this argument are deductive, so the argument is a deductive argument. What about the premises of the argument? Premise 1, "Aesthetic experiences of a fairly great magnitude are always good," is presumably an inductive generalization derived from multiple observations that aesthetic experiences that equal or exceed a certain degree of magnitude are invariably good. The argument is apparently a straight-forward inductive generalization that property A is invariably accompanied by property B. (See the remarks at the end of Section III of this chapter for further comment on this point.) Premise 2 is simply a particular application of the definition of "instrumentally good." Premise 3, "This work of art can produce an aesthetic experience of fairly great magnitude," is not a generalization but a singular report of an experience of the kind used in the support of premise 1, which is a generalization.

There are also other principles available, given Beardsley's theory, that can function in arguments similar to the sample argument just given. Examples of such principles are:

Aesthetic experiences of less than fairly great magnitude are always not good.

Aesthetic experiences of a fairly low magnitude are always bad.

The expressions "fairly great magnitude" and "fairly low magnitude" refer to threshold points that mark the dividing lines respectively between good and not good and between bad and not bad aesthetic experiences.

The sample argument is now complete, but premises of the kind Beardsley mentions as the premises of critical arguments (reason-premises such as "This work of art is unified" and "This work of art is intense") have not been mentioned. Nor has there been any mention of Beardsley's three principles—"A unified work of art always has some value," for example.

It is, however, certainly true that statements such as "This work of art is unified," "This work contains a touch of humor," and "This work is intense"—statements that refer to properties of works of art—are used by critics in connection with their critical evaluations. The question is, Given Beardsley's theory, does he give the right account of the relation between critical evaluations and reason-statements that refer to properties of works of art?

Aesthetic experience is basic in Beardsley's evaluational theory. Whatever value a work of art has derives from the value of the aesthetic experience it can produce: a good work of art is good because it can produce a good aesthetic experience, a poor work of art is poor because it can produce only an aesthetic experience that is less than good, and so on. In order for a critic to know that a work of art is good, he or she must first have an aesthetic experience produced by the work and judge that the experience is good. Once the critic knows the aesthetic experience is good, he or she knows the work of art that causes it is (instrumentally) good, and he or she is then in a position to construct the deductive argument given above that begins with the premise "Aesthetic experiences of fairly great magnitude are always good" and ends with the conclusion "This work of art is (instrumentally) good."

Thus, on Beardsley's view, one does not have to have premises such as "This work of art is unified" explicitly in mind in order to conclude of a given work that it is good. (Such weak reasons could not prove the strong conclusion that a work is good anyway.) One would not even have to be overtly aware of the valuable properties of the work for them to produce the aesthetic experience. So the question of how *inductively* to draw such conclusions as "This work of art is good" from premises that refer to properties of the work plus some generalizations about properties does not arise for Beardsley's theory, despite the fact that he thinks it does.

As noted above, however, reason-statements such as "This work is unified" and "This work is intense" are used by critics in connection with critical evaluations, and it is clear that they have an important role to play in criticism. What is the role that Beardsley's theory can give such reason-statements? No set of such reason-statements together with the weak principles with which they connect can imply any specific evaluation; they can imply only that a work has some value. On Beardsley's theory and instrumentalistic theories like it, reason-statements and weak principles cannot imply that a work of art is poor, mediocre, or good. Only strong principles involving aesthetic experience and statements about a work's capacity to produce an aesthetic experience of a certain magnitude can imply such specific evaluations. The only role that remains for reason-statements and weak principles is that they can be used to construct explanations of why a work is poor, mediocre, or good after it has been determined that the work is poor, mediocre, or good by means of strong principles. Consider this argument:

1. A unified work always has value.

2. This work of art is unified.

3. Therefore, this work of art has value.

Such an argument serves as a partial explanation of why a work of art has the value it has as well as an indication of the source of that value (unity). The total set of relevant reason-statements plus the weak principles with which they connect will constitute the total explanation of a work's specific value, but they will not imply that specific value.

There are, then, in Beardsley's theory three principles that he explicitly discusses and develops and that he takes to be the generalizations involved in arguments that yield specific critical evaluations. These are the principles involving objective unity, intensity, and complexity, but they are weak principles. There are also strong principles implicit in Beardsley's theory, principles that refer to aesthetic experiences rather than to the properties of art. These strong principles yield specific critical evaluations. The weak principles, which refer to properties of works of art, function to yield explanations of the sources of the value of art.

Now that the distinction between weak and strong principles has been drawn, it can be noted that Ziff's theory involves strong principles and that he does not mention weak principles. Beardsley's theory involves strong principles as well as weak ones, although, as noted, the principles he explicitly mentions as principles are all weak ones.

Beardsley's theory, if satisfactory, has an advantage over Ziff's theory where comparisons among works of art are concerned. At least, given the traditional philosophical hopes about the desirability of comparing works of art, Beardsley's theory has the advantage. As noted in the last chapter, it is not clear how, on Ziff's theory, one could compare, for example, a work that is good because it is well worthwhile contemplating with one that is well worthwhile scanning. By contrast, on Beardsley's theory, works of art are to be compared on the basis of one thing—their capacity to produce aesthetic experience.

III. THE MEASUREMENT OF
AESTHETIC EXPERIENCE

In order to use Beardsley's account of critical reasoning, one must have introspective access at a number of points into an aesthetic experience that one is having or has had. There are eleven locations in aesthetic experience as conceived by Beardsley at which it is possible to have experiential access. For each of these locations there is a corresponding scale on which to plot a measurement of what it is that one has access to in a given location. There is a twelfth location and a twelfth scale, but the access to this location is not experiential but inferential. Seven of the scales are magnitude-of-experience scales and five of them are magnitude-of-value scales. In order to make clear what I am talking about, I shall reproduce as Figure 9 the diagram of aesthetic experience introduced earlier with the scales placed at the appropriate locations. I shall represent the scales as being ones that run from zero to one and that are used to measure

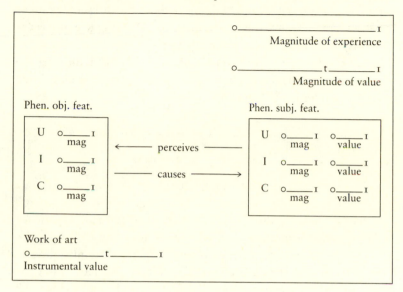

FIGURE 9

continuous degrees as I believe is presupposed by Beardsley's theory. I shall use abbreviations: "U" for "unity," "I" for "intensity," "Phen. obj. feat." for "Phenomenally objective features," "mag" for "magnitude," "t" for "threshold for the application of 'is good,'" and so on.

In order to have a strong principle with the predicate "is good," one must have a sufficiently large number of aesthetic experiences in which (1) the measure on the magnitude of aesthetic experience scale (upper right-hand corner of the diagram) is sufficiently high (toward the 1 end of the scale) in order to be judged to be of a fairly great magnitude and (2) the measure on the value of aesthetic experience scale (upper right-hand corner of the diagram) is at or above the threshold point of "is good." Given this series of aesthetic experiences,one can induce that a fairly great magnitude of aesthetic experience is correlated with being at or above the threshold point of "is good" and advance the strong principle: "Aesthetic experiences of a fairly great magnitude are always good." The two relevant scales (both at the far right top of the diagram), with "x" indicating the magnitude of aesthetic experience and "y" indicating the magnitude of value, will look like Figure 10.

o————————————x———1   Magnitude of aesthetic experience

o————————————t_y———1   Magnitude of value

FIGURE 10

If, in a given case, a work of art produces an aesthetic experience of a fairly great magnitude, this case yields the premise: "This work of art can produce an aesthetic experience of fairly great magnitude." This premise, the strong principle mentioned just above, and the definition of "instrumentally good" yield the conclusion: "This work of art is instrumentally good." The two relevant scales (the first on the upper far right and the second on the lower far left of the diagram) with "z" indicating the magnitude of instrumental value will look like Figure 11.

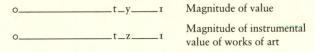

o————————————t_y———1   Magnitude of value

o————————————t_z———1   Magnitude of instrumental value of works of art

FIGURE 11

The magnitudes of the subjective unity, intensity, and complexity (registered of their respective three scales at the middle right of the diagram) each correlates with its corresponding value scale. The unity scale pair (of these three pairs) looks like Figure 12. On this value scale and the value scales of subjective intensity and complexity, there are no threshold points for "is good." This is so because

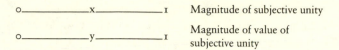

FIGURE 12

it is not plausible that even the highest magnitude of any one of the three subjective aspects could "add up" to a value of "is good." Only the value of aesthetic experience scale and the instrumental value of works of art scale have threshold points for "is good."

Each of the subjective value scales correlates with the instrumental value of works of art scale, and these are the bases for the weak inferences. In these cases, the threshold point for "is good" on the instrumental value scales does not function because it is not plausible that even the highest value of any one of the three subjective values could be sufficient to ground a value magnitude at or above the threshold point on the instrumental value scale.

The three objective magnitudes of unity, intensity, and complexity (on the middle left side of the diagram) provide the causal base for all the inferences (strong or weak), although these objective features are explicitly referred to only in the cases of weak inference.

In Beardsley's theory there has to be a discoverable relationship between the magnitude of an aesthetic experience and the magnitude of value of that aesthetic experience that ultimately provides a basis for the inference to the value of the work of art that causes the aesthetic experience. It would appear from the discussion of the measurement of aesthetic experience above that the relationships between the magnitudes of aesthetic experience and the magnitudes of value of aesthetic experience are to be discovered by introspection; that is, it appears that one is supposed to determine through introspection that an aesthetic experience has a particular magnitude and a particular magnitude of value and thereby establish a relationship between the two magnitudes. However, this cannot be Beardsley's view. He claims that the value that aesthetic experience has is instrumental value and the instrumental value of an experience cannot be determined by the introspection of the experience. The instrumental value of an experience will have to be determined by discovering what kind of consequences result from having the experience. Beardsley suggests in the final chapter of his book that improved mental health and the like will result from the having of aesthetic experiences and that aesthetic experience derives its value from producing such consequences. If one knows which magnitudes of aesthetic experience are correlated with which magnitudes of value of aesthetic experience and one can introspectively discover the magnitudes of aesthetic experiences, then one is in a position to use Beardsley's theory to evaluate works of art.

It was seen in Chapter Three that Ziff's theory does not in the end avoid relativism, for he does not show that it is impossible for two persons performing the same relevant action to disagree over the intrinsic worthwhileness of the actions they perform. It may appear that Beardsley's theory is subject to a very similar difficulty—for can't two persons disagree about the magnitude of value of their aesthetic experience? But for Beardsley it isn't a person's finding an aesthetic experience intrinsically valued that is the basis for evaluating art. For him, aesthetic experience is valuable or not according to its instrumental value in producing some further value—something like general human welfare. For him, two persons disagreeing over their intrinsic valuing of the experience of a work of art is just irrelevant. What counts for Beardsley is whether an aesthetic experience can be conducive to human welfare. I make no claims here about the adequacy of Beardsley's extended instrumentalism and its success in avoiding relativism; I do want to show that it differs from Ziff's view and any other view that ultimately relies on intrinsic valuing.

IV. PRIMARY AND SECONDARY CRITERIA

Beardsley's explicit view is that there are three and only three (weak) principles involved in art criticism—that is, that there are only three properties that are *always* valuable in works of art, namely, unity, intensity, and complexity. The reason why these three properties are always valuable is that they can be instrumental in producing the valuable phenomenally subjective features of aesthetic experience that mirror these artistic properties. Critics, however, frequently cite as merit-reasons properties other than Beardsley's three. As examples of these kinds of reasons, Beardsley mentions humor, lyric grace, and heroic strength. But, Beardsley argues, such characteristics as these may be merits in one work and defects in another or merits in one work and neutral in another. Thus, such characteristics are not *always* merits and, hence, not *general* merits. Therefore, weak principles such as "Humor in a work of art always has some value" and the like are not possible, according to Beardsley. But, if there are no such general principles, how is humor, lyric grace, or the like ever a merit? Beardsley's answer, in an article published in 1962, is:

> Suppose the touch of humor (the grave-digger's gags, the drunken porter at the gate) is a merit in one context because it heightens the dramatic tension, but a defect in another context, where it lets the tension down. Then we may admit that the touch of humor is not a general merit, but only because we also admit that something else is a general merit—(in a play, that is)—namely, high dramatic tension.[14]

There are two aspects to Beardsley's answer: (1) that humor and other such characteristics function differently in different contexts and (2) that humor and such characteristics in one context are conducive to higher order value and in another context they are not. Humor and other such characteristics acquire the generality necessary to be merits by interacting with other features to produce higher order value: the merit-generality of humor and many other characteristics is thus a *dependent* generality.

There are, according to Beardsley, two levels of merit-generality and defect-generality: merits and defects that are always merits or defects all by themselves (*independent* generality) and merits and defects that are merits or defects only in conjunction with other features (*dependent* generality). Beardsley formulates the distinction between these two levels with the following definitions:

> Let us say that the properties A, B, C are the *primary* (*positive*) *criteria* of aesthetic value if the addition of any one of them or an increase of it, without a decrease in any of the others, will always make the work a better one.
>
> And let us say that a given property X is a *secondary* (*positive*) *criterion* of aesthetic value if there is a certain set of other properties such that, whenever they are present, the addition of X or an increase in it will always produce an increase in one or more of the primary criteria.[15]

Notice that these definitions are not intended to help discover which actual features are primary and which secondary. The definition of "secondary criterion" presupposes that the primary criteria are already known because it concludes: "will always produce an increase in one or more of the primary criteria." And the definition of "primary criteria" also presupposes that the primary criteria are already known because it contains the phrase "without a decrease in any of the others," in which "the others" means "the other primary criteria." Thus, in order to apply the definitions to an actual feature one would already have to know which are the primary criteria.

Of course, Beardsley thinks that the primary criteria are unity, intensity, and complexity, but how does he know that these three are primary criteria and that they are the only primary criteria? Of course, he never claims to *know* that they are the primary criteria and the only three. The prominent place that unity, intensity, and complexity have in his account of aesthetic experience leads him to believe that they are of especial importance. He also expresses the belief that all relevant reasons are subsumable under unity, intensity, or complexity either by being disguised under another name (complexity referred to as variety, for example) or by being a feature that feeds into unity, intensity, or complexity. Beardsley, however, never attempts to prove that all reasons are thus subsumable.

To show that all relevant reasons are subsumable under unity, intensity, or complexity and that these three are each independently valuable would involve the large enterprise of showing in a sample of sufficient size that relevant reasons are subsumable under unity, intensity, or complexity and that unity, intensity, and complexity are the only independently valuable features. No one has done this.

I shall return to the question of how many critical principles there are in the next chapter.

V. THE INDUCTIVE SURVEY

The exposition of Beardsley's theory of art evaluation is now complete. I turn now to an attempt to show that his theory has a fatal flaw.

Beardsley claims that the proper experience of art is the aesthetic experience of art (as he conceives of aesthetic experience). Near the end of Section I, I noted that the only possible justification for his view would be an inductive survey of clearly correct experiences of works of art that reveals that these experiences are in fact typically aesthetic experiences as conceived by him. I shall focus here on the question of whether such a survey supports Beardsley's contention that the experience of art has the insular character he claims it has.

Consider the experience of listening to a typical string quartet. The question of moral value cannot arise because such music cannot have a moral content. The question of cognitive value in any ordinary sense scarcely arises either, although Goodman argues for a "cognitive" dimension that we need not concern ourselves with here.[16] Neither the music nor any part of it makes any reference to anything. Neither the music nor any part of it involves any relation of a more general cognitive sort, of a moral sort, or of anything similar to something outside the experience. This musical experience seems to have the detached nature that Beardsley attributes to all aesthetic experience. I think, however, it would be more accurate to say that the experience has a sharply focused nature. (I shall ignore here the question of whether the supposed detachedness of aesthetic experience nullifies what might be called the "background" relations that a work of art has, for example, the experiencing of the music as music of a particular kind. I shall, as Beardsley does, focus on such "nonbackground" relations as cognitive and moral relations.)

Consider now, however, the experience of reading *The Adventures of Huckleberry Finn*. The work of course has the three standard properties that Beardsley attributes to works—unity, intensity, and complexity. But does the experience of the work have the detached nature that Beardsley attributes to aesthetic experience and that the experience of a typical string quartet appears to have? Unlike typical string quartet music, the world of this novel clearly relates to something outside itself and outside the immediate experience of it. The states of Illinois and Missouri are referred to, as are the Mississippi River and the Ohio River. The institution of slavery as practiced in the United States is described in vivid detail. Huckleberry Finn's soliloquy on the raft as to whether he would turn in Jim the slave as he knew he ought to or whether he would allow his companion to remain free is a brilliant depiction of moral struggle. A knowledgeable reader cannot experience this novel without being aware of its moral content and its relations to the world outside it. Such a reader may be completely absorbed in the novel without being detached in Beardsley's sense, that is, without being emotionally distanced or free of the dominance of concerns about the past. The absorption into the world of the novel does not cut one off from the world of history and the present together with their emotional ties. Beardsley, I think, influenced by earlier theories of detachment, mistakes the absorption one experiences in attending to art for detachment from moral and cognitive concerns. Unlike patting one's head and rubbing one's stomach at the same time, there is no mutual interference involved in raptly attending to something like *The Adventures of Huckleberry Finn* and being aware of its cognitive relations and being moved by its moral content. It is not, by the way, the leisureliness of novel-reading that enables us to have the complex experience just indicated; the experience of a stage or movie version of the novel can be just as complex. The recognitions and realizations involved in dealing with the moral and cognitive content of a work are virtually instantaneous. These recognitions and realizations, therefore, need not distract us from our attention to any aspect of the work, although it is admittedly possible that in given cases they might. The experience of art is awash with all kinds of recognitions, realizations, and awarenesses that function at various levels. The most basic is the awareness that the objects we are involved with are works of art. There is also the just-noticeably-different awareness that the object is art of a particular kind. Coping with all of these matters is well within the range of human mental capacity, and they do not in any way generally undermine the experience of art.

There is nothing about the experience of works such as *The Adventures of Huckleberry Finn* that nullifies the relation of any of their contents to the actual world. Indeed, such experience may heighten one's awareness of aspects of the actual world. Since there is no nullification of relations in this kind of experience, there is no justification for the *general* conclusion that the experience of art is detached from moral and cognitive matters and that, consequently, we ought not to concern ourselves with such matters in evaluating art. Finally, it may be noted that one of the prime reasons that *The Adventures of Huckleberry Finn* is regarded as a great novel and better than, for example, *The Adventures of Tom Sawyer* is because of its confrontation of the moral issue of slavery. For additional examples that show the importance of reference for the experience of literary works, see the examples so elegantly worked out by Robert Yanal in "Denotation and the Aesthetic Appreciation of Literature."[17] Several of Yanal's examples will be discussed in Chapter Seven.

Beardsley's theory of art evaluation makes art's capacity to produce aesthetic experience the basis for the evaluation of art. His account of aesthetic experience conceives of it as detached and relationless. Thus, any connection a work of art has to something outside the insulated experience of it must be irrelevant to its evaluation. If, however, Beardsley's account of aesthetic experience (the experience of art) as detached is not generally adequate, then the whole argument collapses. The way is then open for the development of an instrumentalistic theory for the evaluation of art that is not tied to an insular conception of the experience of art.

CHAPTER FIVE

Critical Principles: Sibley

As noted in the last chapter, Monroe Beardsley's account of critical reasoning about the value of art involves a commitment to critical principles, that is, to general criteria. He has devoted considerable time and energy as well as great philosophical skill to combating those who deny that such generality is involved in evaluative criticism. In this chapter, although I shall not challenge the importance of critical principles, I shall call into question the particular view that Beardsley has worked out. In part, I shall rely on an argument recently published by Frank Sibley that greatly illuminates the way in which principles function in criticism, but I shall also examine and criticize some aspects of the view that Sibley offers as an alternative to Beardsley's theory.

I shall begin by outlining Beardsley's arguments and conclusions concerning generality. Although there is a certain amount of discussion of the justification of the generality involved in critical reasons in Beardsley's book, his fullest treatment of the topic occurs in his later article, "On the Generality of Critical Reasons,"[1] where he states and responds to a series of arguments that the opponents of generality have raised against the use of principles in art criticism.

The first argument of his opponents that Beardsley responds to is the claim that there are no single features of works of art "that are either necessary or sufficient conditions of goodness."[2] The word "goodness" in this kind of context can mean either "has value" (weak) or "is good" (strong), but in connection with this first argument Beardsley and his opponents intend the strong "is good." So the question is, Are there any features that are necessary or sufficient for a work of art's being good? Beardsley notes that unity is a necessary condition of having artistic *value* because unity is a necessary condition of being a work of art (as it is of being an individuated thing), but he agrees that there is no single condition that is necessary for being artistically *good*. He also agrees that there is no single feature that is sufficient for being artistically good. Beardsley's response to this first objection against principles is, then, to agree that no single feature is either necessary or sufficient for a work of art's being *good,* but to maintain that nevertheless it is possible that there are single features that *always* contribute to the value of a work of art. Later in his article he calls such features, as noted in the last chapter, "primary (positive) criteria," characterizing them as features that "always contribute positively to the value of a work, in so far as they are present."[3] Of course, at the beginning of his article, he is only asserting the possibility of primary positive criteria; later in his article he goes further.

This first argument of the opponents of principles concerns the conditions of being good and denies the possibility of strong principles, that is, principles that involve single features of works of art that are necessary or sufficient for their being good. Beardsley responds by agreeing that there are no necessary or sufficient conditions of a work of art's being good. He goes on, however, to maintain that there may be sufficient conditions of value—features that always contribute positively to the value of works of art. Thus, he implicitly denies the possibility of strong principles that refer to features of works of art while maintaining the possibility of weak principles such as "A unified work of art always has some value." Beardsley's denial of strong principles here is not inconsistent with the fact that his theory in fact generates strong principles. Here he is denying strong principles that refer to such features of works of art as unity, intensity, and complexity; the strong principles that his theory generates refer to aesthetic experience.

The second argument of his opponents maintains that the same particular feature may be a merit in one artwork and a defect or even neutral in another.[4] From these alleged facts they argue that such features must lack the generality that is required for them to be incorporated into principles. Beardsley's answer is to accept his opponents' contention that a particular feature may be a merit in one artwork and a defect or neutral in another, but he goes on to argue that a feature may be a merit in one work of art because of the way it interacts with other features of the work and be a defect or neutral in another work of art because of the way it interacts with the *different* features of the second work. According to Beardsley, then, a feature may be a merit in one work of art because it contributes to a higher order value but a defect or neutral in another work because it does not contribute to a higher order value. If a feature does contribute to a higher order value *and* the higher order value is *always* a merit, then the feature in question has what in the last chapter I called *dependent* generality. (A higher order value that is always a merit has independent generality.)

The third argument of the opponents of principles is that one feature may be a merit in one work and a different feature may be a merit in another work.[5] Beardsley's answer to this claim is that such merits may have dependent generality through their interactions with other features that produce higher order value (as in the case of the second argument), or the two features may both be *different* higher order values that are always merits. This last possibility requires that there be more than one higher order independent value.

Up to this point in "On the Generality of Critical Reasons," Beardsley's answers to the opponents of generality are entirely conditional. To the first objection, he answers that while there are no necessary or sufficient conditions for being a good work of art, it is possible that some feature or features may always contribute to the value of a work of art. This answer argues for the possibility of independent generality. His answer to the second objection, that the same feature may be a merit, a defect, or neutral in different contexts, argues for the possibility of dependent generality, if there is independent generality. His answer to the third objection, that two different features may be merits in two different works, argues that there is dependent generality (if there is independent generality) or that there is independent generality if there are two features that are independently general. To complete his argument Beardsley needs to show (1) that there are at least two independently general merits and (2) that all dependent merits are merits because they interact with other features of works of art to produce one of the two or more independent merits.

Beardsley formulates his definitions of independent generality (his term is "primary criteria") and dependent generality (his term is "secondary criteria") as follows:

Let us say that the properties A, B, C are the *primary* (*positive*) *criteria* of aesthetic value if the addition of any one of them or an increase in it, without a decrease in any of the others, will always make the work a better one.

And let us say that a given property X is a *secondary* (*positive*) *criterion* of aesthetic value if there is a certain set of other properties such that, whenever they are present, the addition of X or an increase in it will always produce an increase in one or more of the primary criteria.[6]

Two things can be noted about these definitions: (1) they are both concerned only with sufficiency for aesthetic value and (2) the criteria are, in my terminology, weak. Again, Beardsley does not realize that there are strong principles involving aesthetic experience implicit in his theory and that these strong principles involve both necessary and sufficient conditions.

At the very end of "On the Generality of Critical Reasons," Beardsley goes a little way toward removing the conditionality of his arguments. He quotes Paul Ziff's remark: "Some good paintings are somewhat disorganized; they are good in spite of the fact that they are somewhat disorganized. But no painting is good because it is disorganized and many are bad primarily because they are disorganized."[7] Beardsley says of this remark, "Ziff is precisely correct. . . . Disorganization, by this exact description, is a primary (negative) critical criterion."[8] By implication, Beardsley is claiming that being organized (unified) is a primary positive critical criterion. If these remarks suffice, they establish that there is one primary positive critical criterion (unity). However, to complete his argument, as noted earlier, Beardsley needs to establish that there are at least two primary positive criteria.

In Chapter Four it was seen that Beardsley in fact maintains that there are exactly three primary criteria: unity, intensity, and complexity. Beardsley never proves that his trinitarian view is the case, but if it is true, it removes the conditionality of his argument in "On the Generality of Critical Reasons." There is, of course, no logical connection between his definition of "primary positive criteria" and his view that there are three and only three primary criteria; it is possible, given the definition, that there is only one primary positive criterion or that there are two, three, four, or even more such criteria.

There is, however, a problem with Beardsley's definition of "primary criteria." It is a defining characteristic of secondary criteria that they must interact with other features of the work so as to contribute to a higher order value, which itself either is a primary criterion or ultimately leads to a primary criterion. Because interaction is necessary for secondary criteria, their generality is conditional or dependent. In contrast, a primary criterion on Beardsley's view must have the independent generality that is required if there are to be principles at all. As noted earlier, Beardsley characterizes such generality as follows: "The primary criteria . . . always contribute positively to the value of a work, in so far as they are present."[9] Beardsley's definition of "primary criteria," however, does not guarantee independent generality as he conceives of it. Recall his definition: "Let us say that the properties A, B, C are the *primary (positive) criteria* of aesthetic value if the addition of any one of them or an increase in it, without a decrease in any of the others, will always make the work a better one." Notice that the definition contains the qualification "without a decrease in any of the others." The word "others" here must refer to "the other primary positive criteria," and this raises a question of whether one can use the definition as a test of whether a given feature is a primary positive criterion. That is, if one uses the definition to see if a given property, say unity, is a primary positive criterion, one must already know what the other primary positive criteria are. But perhaps this problem can be avoided by applying the definition to a set of properties all at once, say unity, intensity, and complexity. So let us go back to the qualification itself and the problem of whether Beardsley's definition of "primary criteria" guarantees independent generality as he conceives of it.

Unity, intensity, and complexity seem to fit the description well enough. The addition or increase of any of them would, no doubt, make a work better, if it does not decrease any other primary positive criterion. But because the definition allows for *interaction* among the primary positive criteria, there could be cases of works of art in which the addition or increase of one primary positive criterion, say unity, could cause a sufficient decrease of another, say complexity, so that a work does not become better. Beardsley has asserted that primary criteria "always contribute positively to the value of a work, in so far as they are present," but his definition of "primary positive criteria" allows for interaction so that something can satisfy the definition without contributing positively to the value of a work. Thus, Beardsley's definition of "primary positive criteria" does not really accomplish what he wants it to do: it does not really define independent generality as he actually conceives of it.

Frank Sibley opens his important article, "General Criteria and Reasons in Aesthetics,"[10] by acknowledging his agreement with Beardsley about the necessity of generality (that is, principles) for evaluative criticism, but he argues that Beardsley tries to do more than is actually required. Sibley claims that Beardsley mistakenly supposes it necessary to find criteria that, when present in a work of art, always count only in a positive way, the so-called primary positive criteria. Sibley is right that Beardsley desires such criteria, and I believe that Beardsley thinks his definition of "primary positive criteria" realizes his desired goal for he explicitly says, "The primary criteria . . . always contribute positively to the value of a work, in so far as they are present." I have shown, however, that the definition of "primary positive criteria" that Beardsley formulates does not accommodate his desire. Without his realizing it, Beardsley's definition fails to satisfy his goal because it allows for the interaction of his primary criteria and the consequent possibility of the diminution of the value of a work.

Beardsley is led to the desire for ultimate criteria that always, in every work, count only in one way, because, according to Sibley, he fails to make an important distinction. Beardsley, Sibley notes, treats two very different features of works of art as secondary criteria. Beardsley treats such features as "containing many puns," "having a touch of humor," and "having dramatic intensity" as secondary criteria because each may be a merit in one work of art and a defect in another work. Such features, according to Beardsley, are merits or defects because of the way they interact with other aspects of the works. Sibley agrees that a feature such as "containing many puns" requires interaction with other properties to be either a merit or a defect, because "having many puns" is entirely neutral and "carries no implication of aesthetic merit or defect."[11] On the other hand, he maintains that such properties as "having a touch of humor" and "having dramatic intensity" "inherently possess . . . aesthetic merit."[12] Beardsley fails to notice, according to Sibley, that he has collected radically different kinds of features under the same heading. Of course, features with inherent aesthetic merit can interact with one another (and presumably with neutral features) to produce greater or lesser value, but they are not in themselves neutral. There are, Sibley asserts, an indefinitely large number of inherently positive aesthetic merits (elegance, grace, wittiness, balance) and an indefinitely large number of inherently negative aesthetic defects (garishness, sentimentality, bombast, ugliness), and he asserts that "all these are basic or primary aesthetic criteria, some of merit, some of demerit."[13] Thus, the real distinction to be drawn here is the distinction between inherently *neutral* features, which may in given cases interact with other properties to produce value or disvalue in art, and inherently *charged* (aesthetic) features, which may also in given cases interact with other properties to produce value or disvalue.

Why does Beardsley refuse to accept such properties as a touch of humor, dramatic intensity, elegance, and garishness as primary criteria? Sibley maintains it is because (1) Beardsley realizes that such features can be a merit in one work of art and a defect in another work *and* (2) Beardsley supposes that he must find features that *in every work* always count in only one way, if they are to be primary criteria. Sibley maintains that Beardsley's supposition is unnecessary. Elegance, garishness, and the like always have aesthetic polarity, although because of their interactions with other properties, they can be either merits or defects in actual works of art. It is just unnecessary, Sibley claims, to find features that in every work always count in only one way. Also, it is apparently impossible to find the sort of thing Beardsley wants. As noted earlier, Beardsley's definition of "primary positive criteria" fails to achieve the goal he was aiming at. (Sibley does not notice that the definition fails because it allows for interaction of primary criteria—just the thing that he wants.)

There is a way to reformulate the definition of "primary positive criterion" that avoids the criticism made above. The trick is to leave out all reference to interaction within a work of art. The definition then goes as follows:

> A property is a *primary positive criterion* of aesthetic value if it is a property of a work of art and if in isolation from other properties it is valuable.

The isolation qualification is to be understood in the following way: The property being considered is to be considered as if it were the property of a work of art that has only one value property. Please note that the isolation clause of the new definition does not imply that the value properties of works of art are experienced independently of one another. Given this new definition of "primary positive criterion," generality is preserved even though a primary-positive-criterion property can interact in a given case not to increase or even to lower the overall value of a work of art in which it occurs. The definition as I have formulated it preserves generality although the word "always" does not appear in it. "Always" could be placed before "valuable" in the definition to signal generality but it is not necessary and sounds odd.

If unity in itself is valuable, then it is a primary positive criterion. So are intensity and complexity, if they are valuable. Of course, it remains an open question whether these three will turn out to be valuable. And, if these three are valuable, there is the further question of whether they are the only primary positive criteria.

Given the new definition of "primary positive criterion," however, there is as much reason to think that the property "touch of humor" satisfies the definition as there is to think that unity, intensity, and complexity do. Once the isolation clause is inserted into the definition, there are, in fact, any number of properties that fit it and, of course, an equally large number that would satisfy a parallel definition of "primary negative criterion."

Once the definition of "primary positive criterion" is altered so that it will include many of the properties Beardsley wanted to designate "secondary positive criteria," the distinction between primary and secondary criteria of aesthetic value, as Beardsley has made it, evaporates; the new definition preserves independent generality (the goal of the definition of "primary positive criteria") as well as allows for interaction among properties in works of art (the goal of the definition of "secondary positive criterion").

As noted earlier, there is no logical connection between Beardsley's definition of primary positive criteria and his trinitarian view that there are exactly three such criteria, so that the reformulation of the definition of "primary positive criteria" does not have any effect on the trinitarian view. So, even if Beardsley's distinction between primary and secondary criteria must be abandoned, it is possible that he can still hold to his trinitarian view that every merit is an instance of unity, intensity, or complexity, either explicitly or disguisedly, or an element that links up with other elements to produce unity, intensity, or complexity. Nevertheless, it does seem to be a fact that there are a large number of properties that satisfy the newly formulated definition of "primary positive criterion."

With the new definition of "primary positive criterion," there remain two questions unresolved between Beardsley and Sibley. The first question is, Are all properties that satisfy the new definition of "primary positive criterion" either explicitly or disguisedly instances of either unity, intensity, or complexity? The second question is, Are there primary negative criteria that are not merely low degrees of primary positive criteria? Beardsley answers the first question in the affirmative, and will want to argue in something like the following way: Elegance is just a kind of, say, intensity; balance is just a kind of, say, unity; and so on. Sibley can agree that in many cases a value property, for example, balance will turn out to be an instance of one of Beardsley's big three, say, unity. Sibley, however, is skeptical that *all* positive value properties will so neatly sort out in Beardsley's trinitarian way. Moreover, Sibley argues that unity, intensity, and complexity are not "inherently aesthetic at all," but I shall not discuss his contention and arguments at this point.

How important is it that there be exactly three primary positive criteria and that they be unity, intensity, and complexity as opposed to there being a large number of primary positive criteria? If the trinitarian view is true, it would be interesting to know that it is true, but it would be a long, tedious, perhaps impossible task to show that it is true. One would have to show that each of a long list of value properties (elegance, balance, and so on) is an instance of one of the trinity. Beardsley himself never makes a serious attempt to do this. But even if the trinitarian view is true, what does it add to the reason-statement "That painting has value because it is balanced" to say that "and balance is a kind of unity"? As a principle for use in critical reasoning, "Balance in a work of art (in isolation from other properties) always has some value" is just as good as "Unity in a work of art (in isolation from other properties) always has some value."

Of course, Beardsley has a deep, underlying reason for desiring the truth of his trinitarian thesis: in his evaluational theory, the perceptible objective features of unity, intensity, and complexity are supposed to cause the subjective phenomenal features of aesthetic experience, namely, subjective phenomenal unity, intensity, and complexity. The unity, intensity, and complexity of works of art exhibit a symmetry with the unity, intensity, and complexity they are alleged to cause within aesthetic experience. And, presumably, his view (never discussed) is that the value features in the subject must mirror their causes in the object in order to be caused by them. It is not self-evident to me that, even if the subjective features of aesthetic experience are as Beardsley maintains, it is necessary that they be mirror-images of their objective causes. In any event, this deep reason cannot function as an argument for the trinitarian view unless it is worked out in some detail.

In addition to the dispute over the trinitarian thesis and related to it, there is the second question at issue between Beardsley and Sibley: Are there primary negative criteria that are not merely low degrees of primary positive criteria? Beardsley, because of his conception of aesthetic experience and his trinitarian view, must answer in the negative. He must argue that each negative property, such as garishness, bombast, and the like, is a low degree of unity, intensity, or complexity. Sibley can agree that in many cases a value property, such as insipidness, will turn out to be an instance of a low degree of one of Beardsley's big three, say, intensity, but Sibley is skeptical that *all* negative value properties can be shown to be low degrees of the positive value properties of unity, intensity, or complexity. In fact, Sibley argues that there are wholly negative value complexes that are not just low degrees of unity, intensity, or complexity, or any other positive value property, but I shall not discuss his contention and arguments at this point. Again, how important is it that there be exactly three primary positive criteria and that they be unity, intensity, and complexity as opposed to there being some primary criteria that are totally negative and not just low degrees of unity, intensity, or complexity? Even if the trinitarian view is true, what does it add to the reason-statement "That painting is defective because it is insipid" to say that "and insipidness is a way of lacking intensity"? As a principle of critical reasoning, "Insipidness in a work (in isolation from other properties) is always a defect" is just as good as "The lack of intensity in a work (in isolation from other properties) is always a defect."

While I am not persuaded by all of Sibley's arguments, I am inclined toward his view that there are a large number of positive and negative criteria. I do not think that Beardsley's view has been definitely refuted, but its neatness and its lack of support lead me to suspect the view. Furthermore, I am very suspicious of Beardsley's notion of aesthetic experience, and, therefore, I do not find his deep reason involving the symmetry of the three objective and three subjective features within aesthetic experience at all persuasive. My "solution" to the debate between Beardsley and Sibley about the number of primary criteria is to by-pass it, arguing that it is most plausible to follow Sibley's lead. If in the long run it turns out that Beardsley's view is right, it is a simple, logical matter to reduce critical arguments worked out in Sibley's terminology to the neater terminology of Beardsley.

A basic question remains unresolved at the end of Sibley's article: In what way is it justified to claim that a long list of positive and negative primary criteria do, to use his terminology, inherently possess positive and negative polarity? Beardsley, as Sibley notes, has tried to justify his trinity by contending that it is instrumentally valuable in producing a certain kind of valuable experience—aesthetic experience as he conceives of it. Sibley indicates that he thinks the instrumentalist route Beardsley chooses is the right kind of approach, but he believes that the particulars of Beardsley's account are inaccurate. Sibley, however, does not give any detailed criticism of Beardsley's account of aesthetic experience nor does he attempt to work out an instrumentalist account of his own.

Sibley does, however, suggest something that comes close to being for him a test of inherent aesthetic polarity when he asserts, "One cannot intelligibly say *tout court* . . . , 'This work is bad because it is graceful,' or 'This work is good because it is garish.' "[14] Assuming, as Sibley must be doing, that such properties are not neutral, the test shows that gracefulness has positive inherent aesthetic polarity and that garishness has negative inherent aesthetic polarity. (The test assumes that the property being tested is being considered independently of its relations to other properties of the work.)

What I shall call "the Sibley test for aesthetic polarity" is very similar to the "test" embedded in the passage that Beardsley quotes from Paul Ziff's "Reasons in Art Criticism." The passage, quoted earlier, reads as follows: "Some good paintings are somewhat disorganized; they are good in spite of the fact that they are somewhat disorganized. But no painting is good because it is disorganized, and many are bad primarily because they are disorganized." Ziff is saying (I weaken the value predicates),

One must say,

 1. No work will have value because it is disorganized.

 2. Any work will lack value because it is disorganized.

and I think Ziff implies that

One must say,

 3. Any work will have value because it is organized.

Ziff and Beardsley are clearly talking about the same sort of thing when Ziff speaks of paintings being organized and disorganized and Beardsley speaks of works of art being unified, but they conceive of these value aspects in different ways. Ziff seems to think that only relatively high degrees of unity or organization have positive value, and he seems to think that low degrees of unity have negative value. In "On the Generality of Critical Reasons" Beardsley appears to endorse Ziff's view. He says, "Disorganization, by this exact description [Ziff's], is a primary (negative) critical criterion." [15] But this apparently whole-hearted endorsement cannot be Beardsley's considered view, for he thinks every degree of unity no matter how low is positively valuable. Beardsley's conception is to be preferred, because Ziff's view faces the problem of how the same thing (unity) can be positively valuable in one degree and negatively valuable in another. What could be called the "Ziff-Beardsley test of the aesthetic polarity of unity" can be formulated as follows:

One must say (insofar as being organized is considered in isolation from other properties of the work),

1. No work can increase its value by becoming less organized.

2. Any work will decrease its value by becoming less organized.

3. Any work will increase its value by becoming more organized.

Both the Ziff-Beardsley test and the Sibley test are tests for positive and negative aesthetic polarity. However, the types of properties considered by the three philosophers differ in kind. Sibley discusses gracefulness, garishness, elegance, and the like; Ziff and Beardsley discuss unity or organization. Unity or organization is a property that every work of art will have in some degree or other, whereas garishness and the other properties Sibley is concerned with may not be exemplified at all in a given work of art. Unity is a *standard* feature of works of art (and of any other individuated thing), whereas garishness and the other properties Sibley is concerned with are only *occasional* features of works of art (and other things). Complexity, another of the Beardsleyan trinity, is also a *standard* feature; it is a property that every work of art will have in some degree. Although it is not so straight-forward and easy to see whether this is so, the third member of the trinity—intensity—may also be a *standard* feature of works of art.

If unity, complexity, and the Sibley properties have aesthetic polarity, then there are two different kinds of properties with aesthetic polarity—standard and occasional. Sibley has an argument with two aspects to the effect that unity and complexity are not positive aesthetic polarities. He writes concerning unity:

Unity, unlike grace or elegance, is not a criterion that is inherently aesthetic at all. Almost anything may exhibit unity (organization, completeness, etc.): for example, a political rally. But even if we seek unity in what is in fact a work of art, that work may still exhibit a unity that is not an aesthetic or artistic unity. A very bad novel, its episodes thrown together haphazardly, could be unified in the sense that it preaches a single, coherent political doctrine throughout. It may have a unity, coherence, even a developing complexity of political viewpoint, but no artistic worth. But if we have to qualify unity by saying artistic or aesthetic unity, unity itself can hardly be an aesthetic criterion, and, a fortiori, it cannot be a primary aesthetic criterion.[16]

There is an aspect of unity (and complexity) that must be mentioned again at this point. Unity is a property that every individuated thing possesses; it is what I have just called a standard feature. For Beardsley, any degree of unity, however low, is still a positive value. Hence, a very bad work of art with a very low degree of unity (very disorganized) will still have some positive value derived from what little unity it possesses.

Consider the first aspect of Sibley's argument. It is true that any individuated thing exhibits unity, including a political rally, but this does not show that unity is not inherently aesthetic. Things other than works of art—animal movements, sunsets, and even political rallies—can exhibit aesthetic properties—gracefulness, colorfulness, and comicness, for example. For Sibley's argument to work he would have to show that a political rally cannot have aesthetic properties, but a political rally can have the property of being tense, comic, dramatic, or any other of a large number of aesthetic properties. Even if unity is not an inherently aesthetic property, it might be a positive *artistic* value because it is a positive value whenever it occurs in a work of art. Thus, a unity that occurs in art will be a value in art, that is, an artistic value. Further, Sibley seems to be assuming that the only value that a work of art can have is an aesthetic value, but this conclusion requires an additional argument. In fact, I want to deny that the aesthetic properties of the kind Sibley and Beardsley talk about are the only artistic values.

The second aspect of Sibley's argument, involving the example of the very bad political novel, draws too strong a conclusion; such a work would probably not have "*no* artistic worth," but rather a *low* artistic worth. I suspect that Sibley is here thinking in terms of strong evaluational predicates, and he moves from the undoubtedly correct conclusion that such a novel would not be a good work to the unwarranted conclusion that such a novel would not have any worth.

Sibley uses the same argument against complexity with, I think, the same result. In fact, it seems to me that both unity and complexity pass the positive part of what I shall now call "the Ziff-Sibley test of aesthetic and/or artistic polarity."

Sibley has a final argument against unity and complexity as positive aesthetic criteria. He gives the following example as a counter-example:

> A vase might have a variety of ugly features—shape, decoration, color combination—a uniting and mutually reinforcing complex of ugly elements adding up to an intensity of ugliness. Such works, it seems to me, would have unity, complexity, and a resulting intense regional quality—but a wholly negative one.[17]

I grant that the intense regional quality of the vase Sibley is envisaging would be extremely low in aesthetic value. Consider, however, a second vase that has a similar variety of ugly features—shape, decoration, color combination—but in which these various elements are incoherent. Such a vase would have even less value than the one Sibley conceives of. These two cases show that the unity of the vase conceived of by Sibley must have some positive value despite the vase's overall badness.

It is not clear to me whether an argument of the kind I have just given can salvage complexity as a primary positive artistic criterion, but perhaps it could. Intensity, however, is another matter. The vase case that Sibley envisages shows that the intense regional quality of the vase would be "a wholly negative one." (It does not, however, show that the unity that underlies the regional quality is itself negative.) As Sibley notes, Beardsley himself has shown great uneasiness about the possibilities of intensities of regional quality that are negative.

How do things now stand? Beardsley's distinction between "primary positive criteria" and "secondary positive criteria" must be abandoned, but I have formulated a new definition of "primary positive criterion" that preserves the generality he desired for both primary and secondary criteria and allows for the interaction he desired for secondary criteria. It seems that a large number of properties satisfy the new definition of primary positive criterion of aesthetic value and that a large number of properties satisfy the definition of primary negative criterion of aesthetic value. Further, unity is both a primary positive artistic criterion and a standard feature of works of art, and perhaps complexity that is clearly a standard feature of works of art is also a primary positive artistic criterion. We have, then, a kind of compromise between the views of Beardsley and Sibley.

On Beardsley's view, there are three weak positive sufficiency principles:

1. Unity in a work of art is always valuable;

2. Complexity in a work of art is always valuable; and

3. Intensity in a work of art is always valuable.

Also, on Beardsley's view, although he is not aware of it, there are strong principles that are necessary and sufficient such as:

1. Aesthetic experiences of a fairly great magnitude are always good; and

2. Aesthetic experiences of less than fairly great magnitude are always not good.

On Sibley's view, many weak positive and negative sufficiency principles derive from his test of aesthetic polarity. For example,

1. Elegance in a work of art (in isolation from other properties) is always valuable; and

2. Garishness in a work of art (in isolation from other properties) is always disvaluable.

On the compromise view, there are many positive and negative *sufficiency* principles of the kind entailed by Sibley's view. (What I am here calling "the compromise view" should not be taken as my final position. There is more to be added. And I am not sure that in the final analysis I wish to accept all of Sibley's sufficiency principles in just the way I have formulated them. For example, the garishness principle and some others may require qualification.) Among the positive sufficiency principles of the compromise view, there will also be unity and complexity principles.

1. Unity in a work of art (in isolation from other properties) is always valuable; and

2. Complexity in a work of art (in isolation from other properties) is always valuable.

Furthermore, since unity and complexity are standard features of works of art, there will be at least two *necessity* principles:

1. A valuable work of art is always unified; and

2. A valuable work of art is always complex.

Finally, the compromise view has no place for any of Beardsley's strong principles because they depend on his account of aesthetic experience, which is not, I believe, an adequate account of our experience of art. By the way, there is no reason to think that Sibley shares Beardsley's conception of aesthetic experience or his view that the experience of art is detached, but Sibley does not raise the issues in any explicit way.

I conclude this chapter by noting an interesting historical parallel. In the eighteenth century, Frances Hutcheson and Hume, although working in the same tradition, provided a striking contrast. Hutcheson presented a tidy theory in which uniformity in variety is the only property that triggers the sense of beauty, and this single but complex property is wholly positive. Hume, in addressing the same question, gave a long, clearly incomplete list of positive and negative properties that trigger the faculty of taste. Beardsley's and Sibley's theories provide a present-day parallel to the eighteenth-century phenomenon. Beardsley divides Hutcheson's uniformity in variety into its two component parts, adds intensity, and arrives at the tidy view that there are just three primary positive aesthetic criteria and no negative ones. Sibley, in contrast, and like Hume, claims that there are many positive and negative aesthetic criteria. An important difference between Hume and Sibley is that Hume includes many different instances of unity and complexity on his list of properties that trigger the faculty of taste.

CHAPTER SIX

Instrumental Cognitivism: Goodman

I have now arrived at a compromise of Beardsley's and Sibley's views, a view that was expressed at the end of the last chapter in terms of a variety of critical principles. I propose to amplify the compromise view by gleaning what I can from an examination of the recent work of Nelson Goodman.

In 1968, at the very end of *Languages of Art*,[1] Goodman began sketching the broad outlines of an instrumentalist theory that like Beardsley's proposes to evaluate art on the basis of its ability to produce aesthetic experience. He continued sketching this theory in his 1978 article, "When Is Art?"[2] However, Goodman's conception of aesthetic experience is totally different from Beardsley's, and as a result of this difference, a dispute broke out between them.[3] This dispute is a clash between two very different conceptions of the nature of the proper experience of art. Beardsley's view, which is influenced by the Schopenhauerian tradition, conceives of the experience of art as detached and insulated from the rest of experience. Goodman's view, which revives a tradition antedating Schopenhauer, conceives of art as referring to the world and the experience of art as uninsulated from the rest of experience. Goodman's views, as sketchy and undeveloped as they are, are of the very greatest importance, because they challenge the conventional wisdom embodied in the theories of Beardsley and others that the experience of art ought to be detached and that cognitive features of art are not important in the evaluating of art.

The nub of the dispute is whether works of art, when properly experienced, are experienced as referring to things outside themselves. Because Beardsley maintains that aesthetic experience has a detached character, he claims that works of art are properly experienced as the center of a detached experience and that any reference a work of art makes to anything outside itself is nullified during the course of an aesthetic experience of the work. Since the references of works of art are nullified and cannot function in an aesthetic experience, works must be evaluated on the basis of their nonreferential aspects. Goodman, in contrast, maintains that works of art are symbols and, consequently, claims that works of art are essentially cognitive and are to be experienced as standing in cognitive relation to things outside of themselves. Thus, for Goodman, art is to be evaluated on the basis of its cognitive efficacy, that is, on the basis of how well it signifies what it signifies. Beardsley begins with a theory of aesthetic experience as detached and uses it to generate an account of the evaluation of art. Goodman, on the other hand, begins with a theory of art as symbol and uses it to generate an account of the evaluation of art.

Languages of Art's subtitle, *An Approach to a Theory of Symbols*, shows that Goodman sees the various arts as symbol systems. He wants to distinguish the art symbol systems from the nonart symbol systems, and he sees this as the problem of distinguishing the aesthetic from the nonaesthetic. Goodman rejects the traditional ways of making this distinction and makes the novel suggestion that the aesthetic/nonaesthetic distinction be made on the basis of the properties of symbol systems.

Goodman specifies five pairs of properties that symbol systems have. The first member of each of the pairs is an aesthetic symptom and the second is a nonaesthetic symptom. The first pair of symbol system properties is syntactic density and syntactic articulateness. A system is syntactically dense when it "provides for infinitely many characters so ordered that between each two there is a third."[4] Oil painting is a syntactically dense system because each painting is a character in a symbol system, and, for example, given two different paintings of Socrates, it is possible to paint a third that is different from each of the others and "falls between" them. A first painting might represent Socrates as having a large nose while a second might represent him as having a small nose. A third painting could be made representing Socrates as having a middle-sized nose. Between the middle-sized-nose painting and small-nose painting there could be a painting of Socrates with a nose neither middle-sized nor small but in between, and so on. Goodman cites an ungraduated mercury thermometer as an example of something that is syntactically dense and an electronic digital thermometer as an example of something that is syntactically articulate.[5]

The second pair of symbol system properties is semantic density and semantic articulateness. A system is semantically dense when "symbols are provided for things [referred to] distinguished by the finest differences in certain respects." English is cited as a semantically dense system, as presumably any natural language would be. Goodman also cites ungraduated mercury thermometers as semantically dense.[6]

The third pair of properties is syntactic repleteness and syntactic attenuation. A symbol system is replete when "comparatively many aspects of a symbol are significant."[7] An oil painting is replete because all of its features are important, and a chart of daily stock market averages is attenuated because only the height of the line above the baseline is important.

The fourth pair of properties is exemplification and denotation. Exemplification occurs when a symbol symbolizes by being a sample of a property it possesses—for example, a paint chip or a tailor's swatch. By "denotation" Goodman apparently means something like mere reference without any frills such as exemplification.

The final pair of symbol system properties is multiple and complex reference and its opposite. Multiple and complex reference occurs when "a symbol performs several integrated and interacting referential functions."[8]

Syntactic density, semantic density, syntactic repleteness, exemplification, and multiple and complex reference are the symptoms of the aesthetic. By the way, possession of these symptoms has nothing to do with the value of a work of art. In *Languages of Art*, Goodman asserts that the symptoms of the aesthetic "may be conjunctively sufficient and disjunctively necessary."[9] Ten years later in "When Is Art?" he is cagier about the matter, saying, "And for these five symptoms to come somewhere near being disjunctively necessary and conjunctively (as a syndrome) sufficient might well call for some redrawing of the vague and vagrant borderlines of the aesthetic."[10] In any event, all this suggests that if the symbols at the center of an experience have all five symptoms, then the experience is an aesthetic one, and in order for an experience to be an aesthetic experience, the symbol at its center must have at least one of the symptoms. Thus, any experience focused on symbols in English or even on an ungraduated thermometer may be an aesthetic experience, but, of course, it may not be.

Goodman is trying to work out some way of distinguishing those cognitive experiences that are aesthetic experiences from those that are not aesthetic experiences. What all this comes down to is that aesthetic experiences are those in which some attention is focused on the symbols as well as on that to which the symbols refer. How well this scheme works in sorting out cognitive experiences properly, while interesting, is not my primary concern. My main concern is with Goodman's claim that the value of art is to be measured by its cognitive efficacy.

The claims that make up Goodman's evaluational theory are as follows:

1. Every work of art is a symbol which symbolizes by means of either description, representation, expression, exemplification, or some combination of these four.

2. Symbols are for cognizing.

3. "The primary purpose [of art] is cognition in and for itself; . . . [art's] . . . practicality, pleasure, compulsion, and communicative utility all depend on this."

4. Art is to be evaluated by how well it serves its cognitive purpose.[11]

In number 3 above, Goodman's qualification "primary" in saying that the primary purpose of art is cognition and his mentioning of practicality, pleasure, compulsion, and communicative utility suggests that cognition is the primary criterion of art's value but that practicality, pleasure, compulsion, and communicative utility are secondary criteria of art's value. However, Goodman focuses entirely on cognitive efficacy in the remainder of his remakrs in *Languages of Art* and in his later discussions of the evaluations of art.

Perhaps the first thing to note about Goodman's evaluational theory is that it contradicts Beardsley's theory at almost every point. For Goodman, the experience of art is cognitive and this means that it is not insulated or marked off sharply from the remainder of experience. A work of art refers unimpededly to things outside the immediate experience of the work, although this may be a somewhat misleading way of putting it since, for Goodman, the experience of art does not have an "edge" such that things can be inside or outside of it.

Assume for the moment that Goodman is right about art's always referring and being cognitive. How does the artistic value of works of art depend on their cognitive efficacy? One would expect from Goodman at this point a number of examples illustrating the cognitive efficacy of specific works of art. It would be particularly nice to have an example of a pair of works that illustrate how the cognitive efficacy of one is greater than the cognitive efficacy of the other—say, Cézanne's *The Sainte Victoire, Seen from the Quarry Called Bibemus* and Frith's *Paddington Station*. All that is given, however, is a general statement about cognitive efficacy:

> Symbolization, then, is to be judged fundamentally by how well it serves the cognitive purpose: by the delicacy of its discriminations and the aptness of its allusions; by the way it works in grasping, exploring, and informing the world; by how it analyzes, sorts, orders, and organizes; by how it participates in the making, manipulation, retention, and transformation of knowledge. Considerations of simplicity and subtlety, power and precision, scope and selectivity, familiarity and freshness, are all relevant and often contend with one another; their weighting is relative to our interests, our information, and our inquiry.[12]

Lacking specific examples of the way in which the artistic value of art depends on cognitive efficacy, it is difficult to understand and, thus, to evaluate Goodman's theory. Nevertheless, there is a way to evaluate Goodman's claim about artistic value as cognitive efficacy. Underlying his claim about cognitive efficacy is the more basic claim that all art is referential: unless a work of art is referential in some way, the question of cognitive efficacy cannot arise for it. Thus, if there are nonreferential artworks, they cannot be evaluated according to Goodman's scheme. Goodman must show that there are no nonreferential works of art.

The most obvious candidates for nonreferential works of art are ones that come from the domains of nonobjective painting and instrumental music, works of art that are not usually referential in the obvious way that representative, descriptive, and even expressive works are. It is on such works that the controversy between Beardsley and Goodman regarding referentiality focuses. Thus, it is crucial for Goodman to show that nonobjective paintings that do not refer in any of the usual ways (representationally, for example) do in fact refer. Goodman seizes on the notion of exemplification.

Goodman maintains that a characteristic, such as the dominant color of a nonobjective painting, is referential because it exemplifies itself. His contention reveals the radical difference between his theory and Beardsley's: Beardsley maintains a work can have value by merely *possessing* a color that is, say, very intense, while Goodman maintains that, with respect to such a color, a work can have value only because the color it possesses refers by means of *exemplification*.

The issue, then, is whether the aesthetic value of works of art is always a function of the reference of their properties or whether in some cases their value may result from the simple possession of properties that do not refer. (Any value a work of art might have as a result of its expression is being ignored.)

Consider the following five Dantoesque objects: each is a flat rectangle two feet by four feet, each a gorgeous shade of blue, and all are visually indistinguishable from the distances at which they are seen. Three of the objects are paintings side by side on a wall. The fourth, on the floor below the paintings is a bundle of rug samples bound together and labeled "Rug Samples." The viewer sees only the topmost sample. The fifth object is a hole in the wall above the paintings into which an air conditioning duct is soon to be fitted, and through this hole the clear blue sky is seen.

The rug sample both possesses and exemplifies; that is, it both is a gorgeous blue and refers to, say, rug rolls of the same color. The well-established practice of choosing carpets based on such samples makes the reference possible. Beardsley and everyone else agrees with Goodman that exemplification occurs here. That is, everyone agrees that a rug sample is a sample. The painting on the left is titled *The Blue Sky*. This painting is representational and, hence, on Goodman's view symbolizes, that is, denotes. Let it be granted to Goodman that reference occurs here too.

The painting in the middle is titled *The Missing Shade of Blue*. This painting would presumably not be representational, but it does exemplify a shade of blue. The title provides a context analogous to that provided by the practice that surrounds rug selection. If the Humean title seems to complicate things too much, use the title *Cerulean Blue*; it will also supply a context sufficient for exemplification. Let it be granted to Goodman that reference occurs here too.

Move now to the hole in the wall above the paintings. The two by four foot rectangle of gorgeous blue is visually indistinguishable from the other four objects. However, this fifth object is neither a work of art nor a work of rug selection; it is just a section of sky. There can be no question that it merely possesses its color and does not exemplify its color and that it is gorgeous, that is, has aesthetic value. This is a clear case of the aesthetic experience of a bit of nature. Nothing needs to be granted Goodman in this case because no art is involved.

Move finally to the third painting, the one on the right. It is economically titled #*1*. Now, according to Goodman, (1) the blue of this painting exemplifies itself and (2) it is in virtue of this symbolizing that it has whatever aesthetic value it has. It is not clear to me that Goodman has yet presented any argument for the first claim that properties such as the blueness in this nonobjective painting exemplify. What he does do is to talk first about tailor's swatches, pointing out that they exemplify some of their properties (color, texture, pattern) but not other properties (shape, having pinked edges). He then moves on to, say, nonobjective paintings, pointing out that some of their properties are aesthetically important (color, pattern) and that some of their properties are not aesthetically important (being owned by Averell Harriman, being three hundred feet from Michigan Avenue). He notes that the aesthetically important properties of such paintings are shown forth, exhibited, and so forth. He then concludes that the important properties that are shown forth are exemplified and that the unimportant properties are not. Although this conclusion is consistent with what he has said, it does not follow from what he has said. What does follow is that there is something that distinguishes aesthetically important properties from aesthetically unimportant ones. More argument is required to show that that something is exemplification. Goodman needs to show that some kind of context (analogous to the practice surrounding rug samples) surrounds works of art and is specifically responsible for allowing exemplification. That this can be shown seems unlikely to me, especially in light of the fact that Goodman has made no move to do so. It will perhaps be instructive to see Goodman's own words on this point: "The properties that count in a purist [nonobjective] painting are those that the picture makes manifest, selects, focuses upon, exhibits, heightens in our consciousness—those that it shows forth—in short, those properties that it does not merely possess but *exemplifies*, stands as a sample of." [13] This is all by way of argument that Goodman gives. His remark, however, gives no more reason to say that the blue of #*1* exemplifies than to say that the blue seen through the hole in the wall exemplifies. So there is no reason to think that the aesthetic value #*1* has derives from exemplification or any other kind of reference. If #*1* has aesthetic value, it may well be because of the property of blueness it possesses. So, if #*1* has aesthetic value, Beardsley rather than Goodman seems to be right about why it has the value it has.

There is another argument distinct from the one just given that also shows that Goodman's view cannot have the generality that he claims for it. Suppose it is granted that #*1*, and every other nonobjective painting, exemplifies. Granted this claim, would Goodman's view that it is in virtue of exemplification that such paintings have whatever aesthetic value they have be acceptable? Suppose that #1 is a gorgeous blue and exemplifies the gorgeous blue. Let it be granted for the moment that #1 has aesthetic value because it exemplifies the gorgeous blue. #1 must also have additional aesthetic value, because it is visually indistinguishable from the section of blue sky that has aesthetic value without exemplifying. Beardsley maintains that Goodman inadvertently concedes this point at the end of "When Is Art?" when he speaks of the five marks of the aesthetic.[14] Goodman writes:

> Notice that these properties tend to focus attention on the symbol rather than, or at least along with, what it refers to. . . . This emphasis upon the nontransparency of a work of art, upon the primacy of the work over what it refers to, far from involving denial or disregard of symbolic functions, derives from certain characteristics of a work as a symbol.[15]

Goodman's remark about the nontransparency of a work of art and the primacy of the work over that to which it refers implies, according to Beardsley, that works of art have value independent of their references (even if they also have value because of their references). If, however, the mere possession of a property gets any aesthetic value points at all, then the generality of Goodman's theory of art evaluation is spoiled. I was at first convinced by Beardsley's argument, but I am not so sure now. Goodman might claim that the interest focused on the symbol (which is a work of art) is focused simply for the sake of accuracy of reference. But independently of whether Goodman concedes this point, #1 has additional aesthetic value that does not derive from exemplification.

There are two other related difficulties with Goodman's claim about cognitive efficiency as the criterion of artistic merit that are worth mentioning. The first is as follows. Assume that #1 has the value it has because its gorgeous blue exemplifies its color. Consider, however, a second nonobjective painting that like #1 is uniformly colored but is uniformly colored a dull, drab, muddy, brownish-grey. The second painting exemplifies its color just as well as the first painting does, because a painting is supposed to exemplify itself. There is, however, good reason to think that the first painting is superior. Thus, there has to be more to the evaluation of these two paintings than exemplification. Put in another way, according to Goodman's theory, every nonobjective, uniformly colored painting will have exactly the same value if the value of such paintings derives solely from exemplification, but surely all such paintings do not have the same value.

The other difficulty involves types of reference other than exemplification. If cognitive *efficacy* is the sole criterion of aesthetic merit, then the importance of what is signified can have no bearing on aesthetic merit. For example, any two equally efficacious representational paintings will have the same value, independently of what they represent. It is at least arguable that an important subject matter lends value to a work of art, although clearly it cannot be the whole story.

What is it then that makes art valuable? Beardsley and Goodman agree on one thing, namely, that art is valuable insofar as it can produce valuable experiences. That is, they agree that artistic value is instrumental value. I believe that they are right about the instrumental nature of artistic goodness.

Given that artistic value is instrumental value, what conclusions can be drawn about the evaluation of art on the basis of the analyses and criticisms of Beardsley's and Goodman's views that have been given so far?

First, Beardsley is right that some aspects of works of art are instrumentally valuable because they can produce valuable experiences without referring to anything outside the experience of the work of art. Examples of such aspects are the gorgeous blue of #1, the intense combinations of colors in many of Van Gogh's paintings, and the unity of form in a sonnet. Goodman is just wrong that an aspect of a work of art must refer in order to be valuable.

Goodman is right, however, that some aspects of works of art are instrumentally valuable because they can produce valuable experiences in which these aspects are experienced as standing in relation to things outside the immediate experience of the work. Examples of such aspects are the references in *The Adventures of Huckleberry Finn* to specific geographical locations and the depiction of the social and legal relations between slave and nonslave in the pre-Civil War United States. Beardsley is just wrong that an aspect of a work of art cannot be valuable to the experience of that work in virtue of its reference.

Both Beardsley and Goodman suffer from the philosopher's passion for theoretical neatness and simplicity. Each wants a theoretical explanation for the value of art that involves only one kind of feature: *possession* in Beardsley's case and *referentiality* in Goodman's case.

Beardsley's inability to recognize the value of reference derives from the view of aesthetic experience as the only proper product for the instrumentality of art, a view he inherited. The traditional picture of the aesthetic experience of a work of art goes like this: The work and the person or subject who is experiencing it are surrounded by an impenetrable, psychological wall "secreted" by the subject that experientially nullifies all relations that the work has to things outside the experience. Aspects of works of art may, and frequently do, refer, but a "proper" subject of aesthetic experience cannot take account of such references.

The roots of Goodman's inability to recognize the value of possessed properties are not so clear. His view that works of art are symbols, that is, have reference, has something to do with it. There is, however, nothing about being a symbol that prevents aspects of a symbol from having value independently of its symbol function, and Goodman may be admitting this when he speaks of the non-transparency of the symbols that are works of art. If so, he does not incorporate this admission into his theory. Perhaps Goodman has just not reflected sufficiently on the details of his own argument. There is a dialectical tendency that sometimes occurs when a philosopher opposes another view. The attacking philosopher will formulate his position as the exact opposite of the opposing view. Perhaps Goodman is caught up in this philosophical version of Newton's third law.

CHAPTER SEVEN

Experiencing Art: Wolterstorff

In Chapters Four and Six, I examined Monroe Beardsley's and Nelson Goodman's opposing theories of art evaluation. Both view art evaluation as instrumentalist; that is, both hold that art is to be evaluated according to its ability to produce aesthetic experience. However, their views differ radically over the nature of aesthetic experience. Beardsley holds that aesthetic experience is detached and that its content consists solely of aesthetic qualities that are nonreferential. Goodman holds that aesthetic experience is not detached and that its evaluatively significant content consists solely of referential characteristics. Goodman characterizes aesthetic experience as a kind of cognitive experience and correctly concludes that his view of aesthetic experience is diametrically opposed to Beardsley's view. Since Beardsley's conception of aesthetic experience is so close to the traditional, post-Schopenhauerian conception of the experience properly produced by works of art, and Goodman's conception is very different, it is reasonable to think of Beardsley's conception of the experience as *aesthetic* experience and to think of Goodman's conception of the experience as *cognitive* experience. I concluded that Beardsley is right to hold that aesthetic, nonreferential characteristics of works of art are important for the evaluation of art and that Goodman is right to hold that cognitive characteristics of works of art are important for the evaluation of art. This means of course that Beardsley is wrong to exclude cognitive characteristics and that Goodman is wrong to exclude (possessed) aesthetic characteristics as being unimportant for the evaluation of art.

Nicholas Wolterstorff has made a substantial start in the direction of stating a view that synthesizes Beardsley's and Goodman's views, although he does not explicitly mention Goodman's theory. Interestingly, Wolterstorff does not present his view in a journal article or a scholarly book but in an introductory text, *Art in Action*,[1] written for students who are committed to a Christian point of view. The religious orientation of Wolterstorff's book gives it an advantage over both the usual introductory aesthetics texts and the usual scholarly book. Approaching aesthetics from the religious point of view allows Wolterstorff to view works of art from a wider perspective than most aestheticians do. For example, he is concerned not only to give an account of works of art such as concertos, which are played by musical groups for musical audiences, but also an account of church hymns, which are sung by a congregation. By concerning himself with works of art that other aestheticians seldom if ever reflect on, Wolterstorff notices things about works of art that aestheticians frequently overlook.

Wolterstorff's remarks about art evaluation are useful in the present endeavour because they provide a basis for bringing together what can be derived from the two traditions represented by Beardsley's and Goodman's theories. Wolterstorff, like Beardsley and Goodman, conceives of works of art as instruments, but whereas Beardsley and Goodman conceive of works of art as instruments with a single purpose (for producing either aesthetic experience or cognitive experience), Wolterstorff has a more complicated view. He agrees that some works of art are instruments with a single purpose, but he also maintains that some other works of art are instruments with several purposes.

The purpose (or purposes) that Wolterstorff has in mind is the purpose (or purposes) for which a work of art is "made or distrib-uted." One important purpose of works of art, as Wolterstorff sees it, is the "purpose of contemplation for aesthetic delight."[2] In this he is in agreement, to a degree, with Beardsley. In his presiden-tial address, Beardsley gives a definition of "artwork" in terms of aesthetic purpose: "An artwork can be usefully defined as an in-tentional arrangement of conditions for affording experiences with marked aesthetic character."[3] Wolterstorff goes on to characterize aesthetic excellence as follows: "An aesthetically excellent object is one that effectively serves the purpose of contemplation for aesthetic delight."[4] For Beardsley, aesthetic value is the only kind of value relevant for the value of art; that is, for him, aesthetic value and artistic value are identical. Wolterstorff, however, recognizes artistic values other than aesthetic value, for example, cognitive, moral, and religious values. Thus, Wolterstorff distinguishes between artistic and aesthetic value—aesthetic value being for him one among sev-eral artistic values. He characterizes artistic excellence as follows: "A work of art has *artistic excellence* if it serves well the purposes for which it was made or distributed."[5]

No doubt in a great many cases the purpose (or purposes) for which an artwork was made or distributed provides complete and adequate guidance for its evaluation, but there are cases in which this is not so. Consider the French play that Hume mentions at the end of his essay on taste. No doubt the playwright intended it for contemplation for aesthetic delight, and this intended purpose raises no difficulties. The playwright, also no doubt, intended to confirm or instigate religious intolerance in the members of the audience. Suc-ceeding in this second purpose cannot be something that contributes to the artistic excellence of the play; indeed this particular content of the play is, as Hume says, a defect. Moreover, it is also possible for a work of art to have some unintended aspect, part, or content that contributes to its value or disvalue. Thus, although the intended purpose or purposes for which an artwork is made or distributed may provide some guidance for its evaluation, it is the aspects, parts, or contents of the artwork itself—intended or unintended—that are to be evaluated. What Wolterstorff should say, rather than saying that works of art are instruments with a variety of purposes (which limits matters to the intentions of the artist or distributor), is that works of art are instruments with a variety of aspects (which does not limit matters to the intentions of the artist or distributor). I do not think that this change causes any difficulties or forces any other changes in Wolterstorff's theory.

In this chapter, I shall begin by focusing on what Wolterstorff says about the cognitive value of art, ignoring, in the beginning, his major concerns about the questions of the religious and moral value of art. I shall focus on cognitive value because I believe that it is the vehicle of moral value, religious value, and the other values of art, but I shall address the question of the other values of art later in this chapter.

By cognitive features of works of art, Wolterstorff means "the fact that a proposition asserted by means of some work is *true* [or false]" or "the fact that the world of some work is *true to* [or false to] actuality in some respect."[6] A cognitive feature can be a merit, according to Wolterstorff, because we derive satisfaction from noticing either that the world of a work is true to actuality in some respect or that a proposition asserted by means of a work is true. As noted earlier, Wolterstorff's view can be seen as an attempt to synthesize Beardsley's aestheticism and Goodman's cognitivism. I shall focus on two very closely related facets of what I am interpreting as Wolterstorff's attempted synthesis: (1) his view of the *relation* between aesthetic and cognitive features of works of art and (2) his view of the *nature of the experience* of a work of art that has both aesthetic and cognitive features. Although these two facets are closely related, I shall discuss them separately.

Concerning the first facet, the relation between aesthetic and cognitive features, Wolterstorff claims that cognitive features of works of art "cannot ground aesthetic evaluation" because such features do not belong "to the aesthetic . . . character of the [art] object"[7] He says the following about aesthetic and cognitive features:

> The aesthetic qualities of things are confined to the qualities of the looks and sounds of things under canonical presentations. But "looks true" and "looks true to actuality" are never accurate characterizations of how a thing looks, nor "sounds true" and "sounds true to actuality" of how a thing sounds. Accordingly, *being true* and *being true to actuality* are not aesthetic qualities of things.[8]

Wolterstorff also holds that things such as stories, which of course do not have looks and sounds at all, can have aesthetic characteristics such as being dramatic, coherent, and so on.

I shall not consider whether this argument is adequate or not, but the argument does make it clear that Wolterstorff thinks that aesthetic features (which are nonreferential) are distinct from cognitive features (which are referential) and that the two different kinds of features ought not to be confused. With this claim of distinctness I do not disagree. Wolterstorff also gives the impression that he thinks that aesthetic and cognitive features of works of art are not related in any interesting way—although he may not have intended to give this impression or even have thought about the matter. (Later in this chapter when I discuss Wolterstorff's view of the *experience* of aesthetic and cognitive features, the reader will see that the impression he gives of the unrelatedness of these two kinds of features is reinforced.) Although I do not disagree with Wolterstorff's claim of the distinctness of aesthetic and cognitive features of works of art, I want to maintain that as a general account of the relation of aesthetic and cognitive features of works of art the view he seems to hold is an inaccurate one. If Wolterstorff intended the view I am attacking, then my remarks are an attempt at correction. If he did not intend this view, then my remarks are an attempt at extending his views.

First, I shall show that in certain cases, cases that occur with great frequency in the arts, aesthetic features actually depend on cognitive features. Wolterstorff does not, I repeat, explicitly deny the possibility of such a dependence, but he does not affirm it, and his treatment does not appear to envisage such a dependence.

Robert Yanal, in an article published in 1978,[9] provides a number of examples from literature that show that aesthetic features can depend on cognitive features. Yanal quotes from Jane Austen's *Emma* the following speech by Mr. Woodhouse to his daughter: "Ah, my poor child, the truth is, that in London it is always a sickly season. Nobody is healthy in London—nobody can be. It is a dreadful thing to have you forced to live there; so far off! and the air so bad!"[10] Yanal concludes that this passage is comic, that is, that this is its dominant aesthetic character. He also points out that the passage's comic character depends on the name "London" referring to the real London and the fact that Mr. Woodhouse's assertion about London is false because it is so greatly exaggerated. That is, the passage is comic because it contains a false statement about London with which the father is trying to dissuade his daughter from leaving home. An exactly similar passage in a work set at a time when bubonic plague was raging in Europe would have an entirely different aesthetic character, say, tenderness, because the statement about London would be true and the father's assertion not exaggerated. Yanal also quotes a passage from early in *War and Peace* that is both tense and comic because of Pierre's praise of Napoleon before a gathering of Russian aristocrats. The aesthetic characteristics of comicness and the tension both depend on "Napoleon" referring to Napoleon and on the reader's knowledge that Napoleon will invade Russia subsequent to the time of the fictional gathering.[11]

Finally, consider the central event of *The Adventures of Huckleberry Finn*—Huck and Jim floating down the Mississippi River.

Here it is important that it is the real Mississippi River that is referred to, because that river flows between the slave state of Missouri and the free state of Illinois (subject, however, to the fugitive slave laws); moreover, that river flows on into the heart of slave territory. The references to these geographical and political realities contribute to the novel's overall coherence. The realities referred to in this work also underlie the mounting tension that results from the southerly drift of the raft as it is carried farther and farther into slave territory. In this case it is not so much the truth or falsity of the statements in the work about the river or the states that is significant, although they have some significance; it is the mere reference to the Mississippi River, Missouri, and the rest that is significant. The reference to these realities establishes the setting and helps generate the coherence and the tension.

Each of these three examples shows that aesthetic features of works of art—in these cases, comicness, tension, and coherence—depend on cognitive features; that is, without these cognitive features certain aesthetic features would be lost. These examples and countless others that could be cited from literature and the other arts show that the view that aesthetic and cognitive features are never significantly related is false.

I turn now to the question of the nature of the experience of works of art with both aesthetic and cognitive features. As a background for the discussion of Wolterstorff's view, I shall give a quick summary of Beardsley's view of aesthetic experience, for it is Beardsley's theory of aesthetic experience as the experience properly produced by works of art that Wolterstorff is trying to amend and amplify.

Beardsley conceives of aesthetic experience as a very neat bundle; the unified, intense, and complex objective features of the experience are supposed to be causally related to the unified, intense, and complex subjective features, and the objective and subjective features may themselves enter into a higher order unity. The content of aesthetic experience for Beardsley is a tightly integrated bundle of aesthetic qualities and affects caused by the aesthetic qualities. He does not deny that many works of art have cognitive features in addition to their aesthetic qualities; he would not deny, for example, that the name "Napoleon" in *War and Peace* refers to Napoleon. He claims, however, that aesthetic experience is *detached* and that the detachedness of the experience nullifies the connections made by the reference of cognitive features. Aesthetic experience has, so to speak, an impenetrable cocoon that blocks reference and keeps the experience of *War and Peace* as encapsulated as a developing pupa. As Beardsley conceives of it, no unsightly relations (referential or otherwise) extrude from the outer shell of an aesthetic experience; its surface is smooth and unbroken.

As shown earlier, Wolterstorff, unlike Beardsley, grants that in addition to aesthetic qualities, cognitive and other features of works of art can be artistically valuable. This fact means that he could not accept Beardsley's conception of the proper experience of art as simply detached and encapsulated, because a work of art's cognitive features relate it to something outside a detached experience. Having sharply distinguished between aesthetic and cognitive features, Wolterstorff makes the following remark in the context of a discussion of cognitive merit in works of art: "Even when engaged in disinterested contemplation of a work we may derive satisfaction from noticing that its world is true to actuality in some respect."[12] When Wolterstorff considers the experiences of works of art that have both aesthetic and cognitive features, he seems to conceive of such experiences as consisting of (1) an apprehension of aesthetic qualities and the satisfaction that results from this apprehension and (2) a second apprehension of cognitive features and the satisfaction that results from this second apprehension. Wolterstorff seems to think of the disinterested contemplation of the aesthetic qualities along Beardsleyan lines. Thus, it seems that, for him, the experience of a work of art with both aesthetic and cognitive features becomes a *mixture* of detached experience of aesthetic features and nondetached experience of cognitive features. Note that I say Wolterstorff seems to hold this view, but he may not. It may be that he just did not pursue the matter far enough to consider the problem and it may be that if he had pursued the matter further he would have ruled out the mixture view. In any event, a consideration of the mixture view has important implications for the theory of art evaluation.

As a general account of the experience of works of art, the view that Wolterstorff seems to hold is inadequate. An experience consisting of a mixture of detached and nondetached elements has a decidedly schizophrenic air about it, but I shall ignore this problem, if it is a problem.

Wolterstorff's apparent view may be adequate for a number of kinds of cases. In the case of the experience of a work of art with only aesthetic qualities, say that of a string quartet, there is no apparent problem: there would simply be the detached experience of aesthetic qualities. (As I indicated in Chapter Four, "detached" is not the best word to describe this experience; "sharply focused" is better. It is misleading to describe the experience of nonreferential properties as detached; it suggests that there is something over and above the experiencing of nonreferential properties that encapsulates and isolates them. So here "detached" is just a manner of speaking. That is, from my point of view it is a manner of speaking, but not from Beardsley's and perhaps not from Wolterstorff's either.) In the case of the experience of works of art that have only cognitive features (if there are any such works), there would also be no apparent problem; there would simply be the nondetached experience of cognitive features. In the case of the experience of works of art that has both aesthetic and cognitive features and in which these two kinds of features are not significantly related, there would be no apparent problem; there would be genuine, unintegrated *mixtures* of detached and nondetached experience.

If the kinds of cases just mentioned do not seem to present any problem for the view Wolterstorff appears to hold, the kinds of cases cited earlier from Jane Austen, Tolstoy, and Mark Twain do. In these cases, the existence of some aesthetic features depends on cognitive features. Thus, the experiences of the cognitive features have to be closely tied to the experiences of the aesthetic features; *integrated* experiences of both kinds of characteristics are required. In such cases, the experience of the intertwined aesthetic and cognitive features cannot be both detached and nondetached. This seems to present a serious problem for Wolterstorff's view; however, the problem can be resolved by abandoning the notion of the *detached* nature of aesthetic experience. (Incidentally, these kinds of cases, by showing the essential role that cognitive features can play in the experience of art, are additional evidence for the inadequacy of Beardsley's account of aesthetic experience.)

Wolterstorff has himself taken a large step in the direction of abandoning detachment by acknowledging the significance of cognitive and other features in the experience and evaluation of art. It was Beardsley's assumption that aesthetic experience is detached that led him to denigrate the significance of cognitive features for the experience and evaluation of art. The logical step to take, following Wolterstorff's lead, is to deny that the proper experience of any of the characteristics of works of art is detached. Consider that this step has now been taken.

Thus far I have been concerned with the significance of the cognitive features of works of art because some aesthetic features may depend on them. Wolterstorff himself is not concerned with this aspect of cognitive features of art; rather he is concerned with cognitive features that have artistic value quite independently of aesthetic features. He speaks of two such cognitive merits: (1) he claims that "we may derive satisfaction from noticing that . . . [a work of art's] world is true to actuality in some respect" and (2) he claims that we may derive satisfaction from noticing that "a proposition asserted by means of some work is true." His remarks strongly suggest that a work's asserting a false proposition and a work's being false to actuality in some respect are defects.

The true-to-actuality merit is very close to the traditional notion of the merit of imitation. The traditional notion, however, is broader in that it includes imitation or representation of both actual objects and fictional ones, as when a painting is made of the goddess Venus. A painting of Venus could not be true to actuality. Perhaps Wolterstorff's claim could be amended to read, "we may derive satisfaction from noticing that . . . [a work of art's] world is true to actuality in some respect" or is true to some *prior* and *independently established* fictional object in some respect. (It would not make sense to speak of being true to a fictional object that is wholly established by the work of art in question.)

In both the true-to-something cases and the asserting-a-true-proposition cases, what is important is the work of art's standing in a truth relation to something. Truth-to a very mundane thing has as much cognitive value as truth-to a very significant thing, and asserting a true proposition about the least thing has as much cognitive value as asserting a true proposition about the grandest thing. I think Wolterstorff is right that a work of art may derive some value from either of these straight-forward and basic cognitive ways of relating art to the world. For example, a drawing of or a haiku about a common, everyday object will have some value because of its accuracy of depiction or description. Of course, other aspects of such works will be important for their artistic value, and a cognitive dimension is not necessary for a work to have value. Clive-Bellish reactions to the over-emphasis of the cognitive features of art and to the neglect of aesthetic features of art have a corrective place, but we should avoid bouncing all the way to the other extreme of asserting that a cognitive dimension of a work of art cannot have any value. As long ago as the time of ancient Greek philosophy and as recently as the writing of Arthur Danto and Nelson Goodman, philosophers have maintained that a cognitive aspect is a *defining* feature of art. These philosophers are not right, I think, about the essence of art, but they are certainly focusing on an important and valuable feature of art. It cannot be just an accident of no evaluative significance that such an enormous percentage of our art is referential in character.

The cognitive value that Wolterstorff is concerned with—the true-to and asserting-a-true-proposition cognitive value—is value that is independent of the significance of what is referred to. Such value can be called "imitative value."

There is another kind of cognitive-based value that Wolterstorff does not discuss, namely, the value or disvalue that works of art may have because of the value or disvalue of the things they refer to. No notable philosopher appears to have noticed this kind of cognitive value, except Hume. At the end of his essay on taste, in a passage already discussed several times, Hume maintains that the religious bigotry depicted with approval in a particular play disfigures it. In Hume's example the disvalue referred to is moral disvalue, but the general implication of his point is that any kind of disvaluable content of a work of art is a defect in the work. Another implication of Hume's point is that the depiction with approval of a morally good state of affairs in a work is a merit in that work and generally that the depiction with approval of any kind of good state of affairs in a work is a merit in that work.

Hume does not give an argument in support of his view, and I expect that he did not think that any argument is required. It is obvious that many works of art have an integral moral point of view, and it was equally obvious to Hume that one cannot take a neutral stance toward a moral point of view. Anyone who has a moral point of view is bound to evaluate the moral point of view of any work that has one. Thus, anyone with a moral point of view will find the moral point of view of a work of art that has one to be either valuable or disvaluable. An argument in support of Hume's point becomes necessary only in the face of a theory that detaches works of art and the experience of them from any relation to the world, and Hume had the good fortune to live before Schopenhauer initiated such a theory. Those who are unpersuaded by Schopenhauer-inspired theories will have to agree with the Humean view that the moral value that a work of art has is an artistic value. Hume's view can be generalized to say that any value in a work of art is an artistic value, because in the absence of a justified theory that says that, in a proper experience of art we somehow cannot experience or must ignore the moral or other value features of art, we are forced to accredit all the value dimensions of art.

The most general statement of Hume's point about moral value runs as follows:

1. Whatever one finds morally valuable in the world, one will find the approving representation of that thing or that kind of thing in art valuable;

2. Whatever one finds of moral disvalue in the world, one will find the approving representation of that thing or that kind of thing in art disvaluable;

3. Whatever one finds morally valuable in the world, one will find the disapproving representation of that thing or that kind of thing in art disvaluable; and

4. Whatever one finds of moral disvalue in the world, one will find the disapproving representation of that thing or that kind of thing in art valuable.

In his example, Hume is talking about the significance of an approving point of view in art. It is of course quite possible for the representation of a disvaluable state of affairs from a point of view that is neither approving nor disapproving to be of artistic value. For example, the disvaluable state of affairs represented might be of great historical significance. It is even possible for the representation of a disvaluable state of affairs from an approving point of view to have artistic value, although it will be of a mixed sort.

I return now to the cognitive value of art. There are three kinds of positive and negative cognitive value that art can have:

1. *Imitative cognitive value or disvalue,* which derives from the satisfaction or dissatisfaction of noticing that the world of a work of art is true or false to actuality in some respect or that a proposition asserted by means of a work of art is true or false;

2. *Supportive cognitive value or disvalue,* which derives from referential features of a work of art being responsible for that work's having certain valuable or disvaluable aesthetic properties; and

3. *Referent-centered cognitive value or disvalue,* which derives from the value or disvalue of the object, event, or state of affairs that aspects of a work of art represent.

Hume's case of religious bigotry disfiguring a work of art fits into the third kind of cognitive value.

CHAPTER EIGHT

Relativism: Hume

Where does the amplified, compromise view leave us? First, it is an instrumentalist account in which the value of a work of art is derived from the work's capacity to be the source of a valuable experience. The question that immediately arises is, *What kind* of valuable experience do works of art give rise to? I shall run through the answers that the theories discussed in earlier chapters give to this question, and I shall begin, as usual, with Beardsley's theory. This quick survey will serve as a reminder of the point to which the earlier chapters have brought matters. Since relativism is a crucial problem for the theories discussed earlier, I shall also briefly indicate how each of the theories in this survey deals with this problem. These discussions of relativism will serve as an introduction to an explanation of the way in which the amplified, compromise view will attempt to deal with this problem. I shall develop my own view of relativism through an analysis of Hume's struggles with it in "Of the Standard of Taste."

Beardsley's answer to the what-kind-of-experience question is that it is *aesthetic* experience that is valuable. Thus, on his theory every work of art can be evaluated on the basis of how well it produces aesthetic experience—a specific kind of experience that is subject to a more or less measurable magnitude. A painting, a poem, a novel, an opera, or a movie all produce the same kind of thing—aesthetic experience. Consequently, at least theoretically, every work of art can be assigned a specific instrumental value, and every work's value can be compared to every other work's value according to how well the various works produce aesthetic experience. (A general discussion of the comparison of works of art with respect to their value will be given in the next chapter.)

Beardsley's instrumentalist theory is carefully designed to avoid the problem of relativism, relativism being the view that there is no way to adjudicate between some differing evaluations of a work of art. Relativism can occur at two levels: it can occur at the level of the evaluation of the properties of works of art and it can occur at the level of the evaluation of the experience of works of art. Beardsley's view, like instrumentalist theories generally, avoids relativism at the level of the valuable properties of works of art by claiming that the value of a work of art is a function of its capacity to produce valuable experience. What, however, keeps relativism from breaking out at the level of aesthetic experience for Beardsley? That is, what prevents one person from finding the aesthetic experience of a given work of art valuable to one degree or measure and another person finding the aesthetic experience of the same work valuable to another degree or measure? On Beardsley's theory, this problem is not supposed to arise for aesthetic experience, because on his view aesthetic experience is not found to be valuable by persons in the sense that it is intrinsically valued by a person. According to his theory, the value of aesthetic experience that is relevant for the evaluation of art is also instrumental value—its ability to produce mental health. Since there is presumably only *one* such instrumental value for a work of art for producing mental health, if there are differing evaluations, at least one must be wrong. And, since Beardsley maintains that all value is instrumental value, the question of intrinsic valuing by persons never arises on his theory, and, hence, relativism supposedly does not arise for his theory.

Sibley, although he does not directly address the question, must say that the kind of valuable experience that is relevant for the evaluation of art is the experience of aesthetic qualities. Sibley's view, unlike Beardsley's, is not guarded against relativism at the second level, that is, at the level of the value of the experience of aesthetic qualities, and he has not yet taken any steps to guard it. Sibley's view also differs from Beardsley's in that Sibley makes no attempt to conceive of the experiences of aesthetic qualities as constituting a single kind of thing as Beardsley does with his notion of a detached and insulated aesthetic experience. Although Sibley does not raise the issue, his notion of the experiences of art as consisting of experiences of a multiplicity of aesthetic qualities would make the measuring of them a very formidable one. And if the measurement of such experiences would be difficult, the comparison of works of art and the experiences of them would be even more difficult.

Goodman's answer to the question of what kind of experience is relevant to the evaluation of art, although I do not believe he addresses the question directly, parallels Beardsley's, with "cognitive experience" substituted for "aesthetic experience." His evaluational scheme, like Beardsley's, avoids the problem of relativism at the level of the properties of works of art. Goodman avoids relativism at this level because for him the value of the properties of works of art is simply their value to do *one* thing, that is, to be a source of cognitive experience that presumably should be the same for everyone. He, however, does not develop any view about the nature of the value of cognitive experience, so it is just not clear whether his view is threatened by relativism at the deeper level of the value of cognitive experience. Since Goodman's theory involves only *one* kind of experience, he might conceivably have developed a notion of the measurement of cognitive experience and also a notion of comparing the value of works of art, but, in fact, he has nothing to say of these topics. Goodman's theory, while generally salutary, is nevertheless very incomplete.

Wolterstorff's answer to the question under discussion is that the relevant kind of valuable experience is the experience for which a work of art was made or distributed. This answer appears on first consideration to be simpler and less complicated than those of the other philosophers discussed. Wolterstorff's view, however, turns out on examination to be more complex than the other views. For, according to Wolterstorff, works of art are made or distributed for a variety of purposes: religious (for example, hymns have the purpose of enabling a congregation to praise God), aesthetic, cognitive, moral, and perhaps others. In Chapter Seven, I concluded that Wolterstorff's view requires some modification; his contention that works of art are instruments that are made or distributed for a variety of purposes must be changed to say that they are instruments with a variety of aspects. This change is required because some intended aspects can turn out to be defects rather than merits, and some important aspects may not have been intended. Wolterstorff's view can be thought of as a conjunction of aspects of many of the other theories, plus additions of his own: works of art are instruments with aspects that result in experiences of aesthetic qualities (Beardsley and Sibley), of cognitive aspects (Goodman), of moral aspects, of religious aspects, and perhaps of others. Wolterstorff makes no attempt to guard against relativism at the second level, that is, at the level of the value of the experience of aesthetic, cognitive, moral, and religious aspects. The great complexity and differences of the experiences of art on Wolterstorff's theory makes the question of measurement and comparison of such experiences and, hence, of works of art that induce the experiences more formidable than for any of the other theories. Wolterstorff makes no attempt to discuss the questions of measurement and comparison.

On Beardsley's view there are supposed to be two different kinds of experiences—aesthetic and nonaesthetic experience—but I do not think that the other theorists claim that there are different kinds of experience or that one particular kind of experience is the one relevant for the evaluation of art. The general impression given by the other theories, with the possible exception of Goodman's, is that they focus primarily on the experience of artistic properties rather than a particular kind of experience. For the other theories, the experience of these properties does not constitute a special kind of experience, as Beardsley envisages. So, for the theories other than Beardsley's (and perhaps Goodman's), the question of what *kind* of valuable or disvaluable experience dissolves into the question of *which properties* of art are related to valuable and disvaluable experiences. And this question focuses attention on the properties that are the sources of valuable and disvaluable experiences. I now turn attention to these instrumentally valuable and disvaluable properties.

First, which properties of art are valuable and which disvaluable? Part of the answer to this question is those properties that are sorted out by the positive and negative parts of the Sibley test of aesthetic polarity, that is, aesthetic qualities such as gracefulness, garishness, and the like.

But why is it that some aesthetic properties sort out as positive and some as negative? That is, why *must* one say that any work will have value because it is graceful, and why *must* one say that any work will lack value because it is garish? The instrumentalist answer is that it is because properties such as gracefulness are a source of valuable experience and properties such as garishness are a source of disvaluable experience.

But why is it that experiences of some aesthetic properties are valuable and experiences of other aesthetic properties disvaluable? The answer to the parallel question in Beardsley's theory—which is, Why is aesthetic experience valuable (and never disvaluable)?—is that aesthetic experience itself is instrumentally valuable for something else. Beardsley's strategy of arguing that all value is instrumental value and never intrinsic, however, strikes me as paradoxical. It seems to me that, at this point in the chain of argument about value, one simply has to say that the experiences of properties such as gracefulness are just intrinsically or unmediatedly valued and that the experiences of properties such as garishness are intrinsically or unmediatedly disvalued. That is, the experiences of valuable and disvaluable properties are valuable or disvaluable because they are *valued* or *disvalued,* not because they are valuable or disvaluable for something else. In saying this, I do not mean to deny that such experiences might also have some instrumental value or disvalue. It may be true or at least sometimes true that the experience of positive aesthetic properties is productive of mental health (as Beardsley says of aesthetic experience) or some other valuable state of mind, but such remarks just miss the point about the valuable experiences of such properties as gracefulness. These kinds of experiences are valuable for us and are sought by us primarily because we just intrinsically value them; such experiences are in this way basic. If such experiences sometimes or always have an additional instrumental value, then fine, but this is not the primary reason that we value and seek them. The point I am making about the intrinsic value and disvalue of these experiences is not a new one and is, I believe, the same point that the eighteenth-century theorists of taste had in mind when they maintained that the experience of uniformity in variety, smoothness and smallness, or the like is disinterestedly valued, that is, valued independently of anything to which it might be related, including any instrumental value it might have. Thus, the reason that gracefulness has a positive aesthetic polarity is that human beings intrinsically value the experience of gracefulness, and the reason that garishness has a negative aesthetic polarity is that human beings intrinsically disvalue the experience of garishness. In general, the same goes for the other properties that have aesthetic polarity: they have positive or negative aesthetic polarity because human beings either value or disvalue them intrinsically.

Another part of the answer to the question of which properties of art are valuable and disvaluable is that any properties that are sorted out by what I called the "Ziff-Beardsley test of aesthetic polarity" are valuable, for example, unity and, perhaps, complexity. The Sibley test and the Ziff-Beardsley test are no doubt really the same test, or rather the Ziff-Beardsley test is the application of the positive part of the Sibley test to *standard* features of works of art. I have treated them as two tests only because of Sibley's reservation about unity as an aesthetic property. So the properties of art that are valuable or disvaluable include the aesthetic properties plus unity and perhaps complexity or, put otherwise, include the aesthetic properties that encompass unity and perhaps complexity.

The above discussion of valuable properties of art has centered on aesthetic properties. A still further part of the answer to the question of which properties of art are valuable and disvaluable goes beyond aesthetic properties. There are many nonaesthetic properties of art that are either valuable or disvaluable. Hume's example of the French play's property of approvingly presenting religious bigotry is an example of a nonaesthetic disvaluable artistic property. At the end of the last chapter I detailed four ways in which moral properties of art, depending on how they are approvingly or disapprovingly presented, can be valuable or disvaluable.

An even further part of the answer to the question of which properties of art are valuable and disvaluable goes beyond both aesthetic and moral properties; cognitive properties are also valuable or disvaluable. Earlier, I distinguished three kinds of cognitive value/ disvalue in art: imitative, supportive, and referent-centered.

Referent-centered cognitive value/disvalue involves the representation of valuable and disvaluable things. The value/disvalue of moral properties of art is a kind of referent-centered value/disvalue. And, as is the case for the moral properties of art, the value of the other referent-centered cognitive features does not derive from the intrinsic valuing of the experiencing of those features by persons. So the basis of referent-centered cognitive value differs from that of the value of aesthetic properties; the basis of the value of aesthetic properties is the intrinsic valuing by persons of the experiences of aesthetic properties, but the basis of the value of referent-centered cognitive value is the value of the thing represented. For example, the aesthetic properties of the play that Hume talks about are valuable or disvaluable because the experiences of them are intrinsically valued or disvalued, but the approving representation of religious bigotry is disvaluable because the thing it represents—religious bigotry— is disvaluable. Thus, the disvalue of the experience of the approving representation of religious bigotry ultimately derives from the disvalue of religious bigotry. So the experience of referent-centered aspects of art has value or disvalue but unlike the experience of aesthetic properties it is derivative value. The value of aesthetic properties flows from the value of experiencing them. Referent-centered cognitive value involves a reverse flow; the value of experiencing referent-centered cognitive value flows from the value of the thing referred to. (I take no stand as to what accounts for the value of the valuable thing referred to.) The difference between these two can be illustrated by Figure 13.

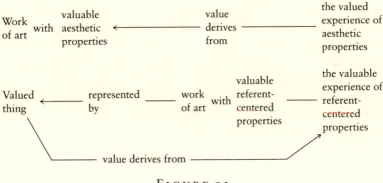

FIGURE 13

Supportive cognitive value/disvalue occurs when referential features of art are responsible for a work's having valuable or disvaluable aesthetic properties. Since the value of aesthetic properties derives from the intrinsic valuing of the experience of them by persons, supportive cognitive value ultimately depends on intrinsic valuing by persons.

Imitative cognitive value/disvalue occurs when there is satisfaction or dissatisfaction from the noticing that the world of a work of art is true or false to actuality in some respect or that a proposition asserted by means of a work is true or false. This kind of cognitive value does not depend on (is not derivative from) the value or disvalue of a referent, and in fact the referent may be value-neutral. This kind of cognitive value is also not derivative in the sense that value derives from the support of valuable aesthetic properties of art by cognitive features, as is the case with supportive cognitive value. The basis for imitative cognitive value, like the value of aesthetic properties, is intrinsic valuing by persons of an experience, that is, the valuing involved in persons taking satisfaction in the truth to actuality or the truth asserted by the cognitive features of a work of art.

How is the theory being developed here to avoid relativism? As noted earlier, Beardsley's theory avoids the problem of relativism, but his view is not satisfactory. The other present-day theories are not and cannot be guarded against relativism in the way that Beardsley's theory is. The problem is this: the other present-day theories claim or appear to claim that some or all of the relevant valuable properties of art are valuable because they are a source of intrinsically valued experience, but nothing in any of the theories shows how the intrinsically valued experience of one person is to be weighted against the intrinsically valued experience of another person. The problem becomes acute when persons intrinsically value the experience of the same property or properties differently. So even if it is agreed that it is the properties of art that are valuable and a compromise is reached about the range of properties that are valuable, relativism still threatens the experiences of at least some of these properties.

The first thing to note so far as the threat of relativism is concerned is that the properties discussed above are not equally threatened. Aesthetic properties are valuable or disvaluable because the experiences of them are intrinsically or unmediately valued or disvalued, and it is possible for persons to value differently. Therefore, relativism threatens aesthetic properties. But moral properties of art have a different status. The moral properties of art are not valuable or disvaluable because the experiences of them are intrinsically valued as, for example, the experience of gracefulness is. The moral properties of art are valuable and disvaluable because they are representations of things that in life are morally valuable or disvaluable. (The point of view from which such representations are presented has, as has been shown, an important bearing on this value.) It is not the responsibility of the theory of art evaluation to explain how and why things are morally valuable and disvaluable in life. It is sufficient for present purposes to note that moral properties in art are not valuable or disvaluable simply because we value or disvalue the experience of them intrinsically, that is, value or disvalue them independently of their relation to other things. I am not claiming that there can be no dispute about moral situations in art (or in life), but I am saying that the value of the moral properties of art is determined in a different way from the way in which the value of aesthetic properties is determined. But if moral properties and referent-centered properties generally are not threatened by relativism within the domain of art criticism, aesthetic properties, supportive cognitive features, and imitative cognitive properties are.

The strategy used to avoid relativism for aesthetic properties by Francis Hutcheson is to claim that one and only one (aesthetic) property (uniformity in variety) is relevant for the beauty of a work of art and that any differing preference is a deviant result of either physical defect or the association of ideas. On his view, preference is nativistically tied to one specific property; that is, human beings are determined by their constitutions to value intrinsically one and only one property. Furthermore, the property—uniformity in variety—that Hutcheson declares to be the object of taste is completely secure as a valuable property of art. Hutcheson is, of course, aware that people disagree in their preferences, but he tries to account for this in terms of either physical defect (physical defect can prevent the correct perception of properties) or association of ideas (the association of ideas can divert one's attention from its proper native preference for uniformity in variety by causing an agent to react to some other property). He thus avoids relativism because if two persons disagree about the beauty of a work of art with the first reacting to its uniformity in variety and the second reacting to some other property, then the second person is deviant because of physical defect or the association of ideas. Thus, Hutcheson's theory, like Kant's theory, confers the nonrelativistic right to speak with a universal voice demanding that others take pleasure in the object of taste. One difficulty with Hutcheson's view is that it is not clear how one can know that *only* uniformity in variety is nativistically preferred by normal human beings. An additional difficulty with Hutcheson's contention that uniformity in variety is the sole value is that it ignores a great deal of what is valuable in art.

The amplified, compromise view being developed here, however, cannot avail itself of the Hutchesonian solution to relativism, for it claims that in addition to the experience of uniformity in variety, the experiences of many other artistic properties are intrinsically or otherwise valued, properties not all of which are as obviously secure as uniformity in variety. Furthermore, the sheer number of valuable and disvaluable artistic properties makes it implausible to think that there will be general agreement about what is valuable and disvaluable. This more complex view, the partial basis of which is intrinsic valuing, is derived from the theories of Beardsley, Sibley, Goodman, and Wolterstorff. Sibley, Goodman, and Wolterstorff make no attempt to deal with the problem of relativism, and Beardsley's view is unsatisfactory. Hume, whose view is also based in part on intrinsic valuing, however, makes a sustained attempt to deal with relativism in "Of the Standard of Taste," and it turns out that Hume's view is very similar to the amplified, compromise view. So if Hume's attempt to resolve the problem of relativism for his theory is satisfactory, it will suffice for the amplified, compromise view. By the way, everything that Hume has to say concerning qualified judges as the solution to the problem of relativism is, I think, directed at the problem as it concerns aesthetic properties of art. He does not connect the moral properties of art he discusses at the end of his essay (or any other referent-centered properties) to his discussion of qualified judges.

Hume proceeds in the same way that Sibley and Wolterstorff do —by listing valuable properties of art. He also proceeds in the same instrumentalistic way to see such properties as being valuable because they are a source of valuable experience; as Hume puts it, "Some particular forms or qualities, from the original structure of the internal fabric, are calculated to please, and others to displease." But as Hume notes at the beginning of his essay, there is sometimes disagreement over which forms and qualities please and displease, so he finishes the sentence by saying, "and if they [the forms or qualities] fail of their effect in any particular instance, it is from some apparent defect or imperfection in the organ."[1] But if the forms or qualities can fail to have their effect on occasion, then Hume's theory is threatened by relativism in exactly the same way as is Sibley's, Wolterstorff's, or any other theory that is ultimately founded on the intrinsic valuing of persons. Hume tries to meet the threat of relativism by shifting the focus of inquiry from the experience of the valuable and disvaluable forms or qualities to the question of *whose* experience of valuable and disvaluable properties is to count in the evaluating of art, concluding that it is the experience of qualified judges or critics that is relevant for such evaluation. Hume's theory, unlike Beardsley's but like Sibley's and Wolterstorff's, ultimately rests on the intrinsic valuing of persons. Hume, however, goes on to specify that it is the intrinsic valuing of qualified judges that is important. If Hume's solution works, it will also serve as a solution for Sibley's, Wolterstorff's, or any relevantly similar theory. Hume's remarks will be a complete solution to the problem of relativism, however, only if the notion of qualified judges can be developed without difficulty *and* the qualified judges themselves cannot or do not value differently.

Reflection on Hume's passage concerning the pleasing and displeasing nature of "forms or qualities" indicates that there are two separate but causally connected sorts of things involved—(1) "forms or qualities" and (2) reactions to them (being pleased or displeased) —and that each raises a question that requires treatment. The questions are, (1) How can one know if a candidate for qualified judge is trustworthy in the detection of some particular form or quality; that is, how can one know if the candidate judge is *cognitively reliable*? and (2) Once one is satisfied that a candidate judge is cognitively reliable, how can one know that his or her being pleased or displeased with what he or she senses is not deviant; that is, how can one know if the candidate judge is *affectively reliable*?

Are there such judges? And if there are, how can one identify them? Hume appears to think that there are such judges and that we can identify them. He begins his account of the method of finding qualified judges with the parable of Sancho's kinsmen. In the story, Sancho's kinsmen are asked to taste the wine from a particular hogshead and evaluate its quality. One says the wine is good except for a slight taste of leather and the other judges the wine good except for a slight taste of iron. Their judgments are derided by the others, who detect no taste of leather or iron, but when the hogshead is emptied it is found to contain an iron key with a leathern thong attached to it. Sancho's kinsmen are the analogs of qualified judges in the arts, and the discovery of the key with the leathern thong (which proves to the ordinary wine drinkers that Sancho's kinsmen are qualified wine tasters) is the analog of whatever it is that proves that a judge is qualified with regard to a particular art. It is clear how the discovery of the key with the leathern thong proves what it proves, but what is its analog in the experience and criticism of the arts? Hume does not appear to tell us. What he does do is give a long account of the characteristics that such a judge in the arts must have. At the end of this well-known discussion, Hume summarizes as follows: "Strong sense, united to delicate sentiment, improved by practice, perfected by comparison, cleared of all prejudice, can alone entitle critics to this valuable character; and the joint verdict of such, whenever they are to be found, is the true standard of taste and beauty."[2] What Hume says is good sense and no doubt as correct a description of a qualified judge as can be given. Hume's description of a qualified judge, however, does not help identify qualified judges for the ordinary person in the arts in the practical way that the discovery of the key with the leathern thong identifies Sancho's kinsmen as wine experts for the ordinary wine tasters.

Hume is aware of the unresolved practical problem, for immediately after the above-quoted summary he writes, "But where are such critics to be found? By what marks are they to be known? How distinguish them from pretenders? These questions are embarrassing; and seem to throw us back into the same uncertainty, from which, during the course of this essay, we have endeavoured to extricate ourselves."[3] Hume, empirically minded as always, goes on to say that, after all, the discovery of qualified judges is a matter of fact and is therefore not so difficult a matter. His remarks do not, however, appear to give us any practical guidance toward the discovery of the critical equivalent of the key with the leathern thong. There is, nevertheless, one isolated and undeveloped sentence buried in the middle of his remarks that is the key to the discovery of qualified judges. Hume's key is this: "Many men, when left to themselves, have but a faint and dubious perception of beauty, who yet are capable of relishing any fine stroke, which is pointed out to them."[4] The fact that a person can come to see, hear, understand, and so on some property *when it is pointed out to him or her* is (or almost is) the critical analog of the key with the leathern thong. When someone can point out to me some feature of a work of art of which I was unaware but which I can then come to see, hear, understand, and so on, then I have the best evidence I could possibly have that that person is, if not a fully qualified judge, then at least more qualified than I am and someone to whom I ought to pay attention. By repeated application of Hume's key, one can discover more or less qualified critics. These judges will not of course necessarily exemplify all of Hume's abstract criteria; in fact, it is virtually certain that, from the point of view of Hume's criteria, the judges we actually find will be flawed. (Notice that in Hume's parable Sancho's kinsmen are not fully qualified wine tasters either, because the one who noticed the iron taste missed the leather taste and the one who noticed the leather taste missed the iron taste. Furthermore, the ability to detect the taste of iron and leather are not the taste abilities one normally associates with expert wine tasters.) The particular virtue of the critics we find using this method is that they show us things of which we were unaware but which we can come to verify in our own experience. Hume's key appears to be the way to undermine the fear of critical skepticism.

But can Hume's key in criticism rid us completely of critical skepticism? Return to the story of Sancho's kinsmen. Suppose there is a third kinsman who pronounces the wine good except for a slight taste of brass, but no one else can detect this taste, and no brass object is discovered alongside the iron key with the leathern thong when the hogshead is emptied. The bystanders and the first two kinsmen have no reason to say that the third kinsman is a qualified wine taster in the absence of the discovery of a brass object, but they cannot say that he is a pretender either because he might be detecting a taste beyond their sensitivities. In fact, Hume's key in criticism is not an exact parallel to the discovery of the key with the leathern thong. The discovery of the key with the leathern thong can do two things: it can enable people who wholly lack a certain sensitivity to judge that a quality is present that they cannot sense, and it can stimulate people who actually have the relevant sensitivity to try harder and actually come to sense a taste of iron or leather. Hume's key in criticism works only when a person has a sensitivity that can be awakened by a critic; it cannot enable persons who wholly lack a certain sensitivity to judge that a quality is present that they cannot sense. So the discovery of the key with the leathern thong does more in its domain than Hume's key does in the realm of criticism. The third kinsman, the one who claims to detect a taste of brass, is more like a critic of the arts, for he has no object like the key with the leathern thong to prove him right. The third kinsman can only hope that his remark will help others who actually have the relevant sensitivity to try harder and come to notice the taste of brass. But Hume's key, like the third kinsman, can go a good ways and does what can be done; it can enable persons who have capacities to realize them.

Hume's key also goes a long way toward defusing the charge of vicious circularity that many have felt that his qualified judge view leaves him open to, for it gives a way for someone to verify in his or her own experience that a critic is qualified. But Hume's key is not a complete solution to the problem of certifying qualified judges because (1) there will always be persons who cannot grasp what is being pointed out to them and hence cannot produce the experience that for them would certify a critic as qualified (the problem of the noncomprehender) and (2) there is always the chance that the candidate judge is not really pointing at anything when he says he is (the problem of the pretender). (If there were exact critical analogs of the key with the leathern thong, these two problems would evaporate.) The problem of the noncomprehender can be reduced somewhat by disqualifying some of the noncomprehenders: the color-blind, the tone deaf, and persons with other cognitive handicaps can be shown that they are defective if they do not already know it, thereby disqualifying them in their own eyes. The color-blindness tests and similar tests that can be used here are like the discovery of the key with the leathern thong. The problem of pretenders can also be reduced to a certain extent. If the candidate judge is unable to show anyone what he or she alleges to experience, then he or she is disqualified and shown to be a pretender. Of course, the problems of the noncomprehender and the pretender cannot be completely defeated; it is always possible for there to be cases in which the noncomprehender does not have any evidence at all that there is something he or she is not comprehending, and there may be cases in which the candidate judge is experiencing something that no one else is and is therefore no pretender. Noncomprehenders can be safely ignored if they are isolated in the sense that many others claim to experience what they cannot experience. Critics who are not pretenders because they in fact experience something that no one else does can also be safely ignored; if what they sense is that rare and difficult to experience, it cannot have the general significance that properties of art must have. So Hume is no doubt right that the (cognitive) problems involved in certifying qualified judges are for all practical purposes resolvable, even if pockets of Cartesian-like skepticism remain. By the way, Hume's account of the cognitive reliability of qualified judges, although he extends it somewhat, is a detailed working out of what is implicit in Hutcheson's remarks about deviant preferences due to physical defect.

Hume's key, however, addresses only one of the two questions raised by his theory; it helps with the problem of the cognitive reliability of a judge, but it leaves the question of the affective reliability untouched. And there is in Hume's essay nothing comparable to Hume's key that can help with the problem of the affective reliability of qualified judges; there is, for example, nothing in Hume's essay comparable to Hutcheson's attempt to use the association of ideas as an explanation of how preference can be perverted. In fact, what Hume does say that touches on the subject of affective reliability undermines that notion. Near the end of the essay, he writes:

But notwithstanding all our endeavours to fix a standard of taste, and reconcile the discordant apprehensions of men, there still remain two sources of variation, which are not sufficient indeed to confound all the boundaries of beauty and deformity, but will often serve to produce a difference in the degrees of our approbation or blame. The one is the different humours of particular men; the other, the particular manners and opinions of our age and country.[5]

Hume in effect withdraws his conclusion about "the particular manners and opinions of our age" being a real problem, for shortly he says, "A man of learning and reflection can make allowance for these peculiarities of manners; but a common audience can never divest themselves so far of their usual ideas and sentiments, as to relish pictures which in no wise resemble them."[6] The first part of Hume's sentence withdraws the earlier conclusion about the peculiar manners and opinions, and the second part of the sentence actually has no effect because the question does not rest upon actual audience reaction, but upon how an audience could be brought to react by pointing out the irrelevance of differing manners, or at least upon how an audience could be brought to agree that they ought to react in a certain way even if in fact they did not so react. The problem of the particular manners is resolvable because it has a large cognitive component. The problem of the different humors of particular men, however, is different; it appears to be a real stumbling block to a universal standard of taste, for it is here that the problem of affective reliability has its base. Hume writes on the matter as follows:

Where there is . . . a diversity in the internal frame or external situation as is entirely blameless on both sides, and leaves no room to give one the preference above the other; in that case a certain degree of diversity in judgement is unavoidable, and we seek in vain for a standard, by which we can reconcile the contrary sentiments.[7]

By blameless diversity Hume means diversity that does not arise from lack of strong sense, delicate sentiment, or the like, that is, does not arise from some cognitive deficiency. The following are some of the instances that Hume cites of blameless diversity:

> A young man, whose passions are warm, will be more sensibly touched with amorous and tender images, than a man more advanced in years, who takes pleasure in wise, philosophical reflections concerning the conduct of life and moderation of passions. . . . One person is more pleased with the sublime; another with the tender; a third with raillery. . . . The ear of this man is entirely turned towards conciseness and energy; that man is delighted with a copious, rich, and harmonious expression. Simplicity is affected by one; ornament by another.[8]

Note that in these instances cognitive issues are not the focus of attention and that Hume is entirely concerned with affective matters; the verbs he uses are "sensibly touched," "takes pleasure in," "pleased," "is . . . turned towards," "is delighted with," and "affected by." Hume is here talking about what I have been calling intrinsic valuing.

Through the bulk of his essay Hume combats relativism on the cognitive front, but at the end of the essay, when he turns his attention to affective matters, he quickly gives in to relativism. Why does Hume capitulate and should he?

Should Hume's resolution be thought of as a capitulation, a defeat, a giving in to relativism? The reason that we tend to feel that it is, is that the objective intrinsic theory of art evaluation, as noted in the introductory chapter, acts as a model of what the theory of art evaluation ought to be and do, even for those who do not accept this view, and, on this view, relativism is just not possible. According to this view, a work of art's being valuable is simply a matter of its having the value property beauty in some degree or other. The greater the degree of beauty, the greater the value of the art. On this view,

"This work of art is valuable"

means

"This work of art has the property beauty."

Relativism cannot arise because, if two persons disagree about whether a work of art has the property of beauty or about the degree of the property, at least one of them will be wrong. Disagreements about value, thus, do not pose a relativistic threat to the objective intrinsic theory. Furthermore, on this view, affective matters play no role in the evaluating of art; someone's intrinsically valuing or disvaluing the properties of a particular work of art makes no difference to the value of that work. This view keeps the value of art and the intrinsic valuing of human beings separate. In the eighteenth century, the theory of taste made affection or intrinsic valuing an integral part of the evaluation of art. As a result of the introduction of intrinsic valuing, which allows for the possibility of different persons valuing differently, relativism becomes difficult to avoid. Hutcheson, as noted earlier, tries to control the effect of intrinsic valuing and thereby to contain relativism by claiming that only one objective property—uniformity in variety—is relevant for the value of art. On Hutcheson's view,

"This work of art is valuable"

means

"This work of art has the property uniformity in variety that causes human beings to value it intrinsically."

This equivalence amounts to the claim that only uniformity in variety can cause human beings unmediatedly to value art. How is Hutcheson to explain the cases in which persons do not intrinsically value a work despite its uniformity in variety and cases in which persons intrinsically value a work with less uniformity in variety more than a work with greater uniformity in variety? Hutcheson's solution to this difficulty is to claim that such cases are due to one or the other of two deficiencies in human beings. (1) A deviant valuing may result from some perceptual (physical) defect that distorts a person's understanding of a situation. Or (2) the intrinsic valuing of anything except uniformity in variety or the intrinsic valuing of a lesser uniformity in variety over a greater uniformity in variety may be the deviant result of the distorting effect of the association of ideas, which diverts the sense of beauty from the thing to which it is nativistically attached. If it is granted, as Hutcheson claims, that only uniformity in variety is relevant to the value of art, then his attempt to avoid relativism works quite well. For, if only this one property is really responsible for the value in art, then it would be deviant not to value it or to value a lesser amount of it over a greater amount of it. If Hutcheson is correct that art has only one valuable property, then relativism can be contained and disagreements over the value of art can be explained in a straight-forward way. The great difficulty with Hutcheson's solution, as noted earlier, is that it fails to take account of many valuable aesthetic properties of art other than uniformity in variety as well as the nonaesthetic properties of art. Hume and other later writers recognized the difficulty with Hutcheson's view and tried to remedy it by acknowledging that art has many different valuable properties. But when it is recognized that art's value derives from an indefinitely large number of different properties, the futility of trying to show that all disagreements over the value of artistic properties have their source in deviance due to either physical defect or the association of ideas becomes apparent. With so many different valuable and disvaluable properties available in so many different works of art, it is not at all surprising that a given work of art will produce a more highly valued experience in one person than in another. When it is seen that different evaluations of works of art arise because of the great number of possible things to value, it will also be seen that only some of these cases can be explained as the result of physical defect or the association of ideas. There are just too many valuable and disvaluable things available to expect agreement. If there were only one valuable thing where art is concerned—beauty, uniformity in variety, or some such—then there would be no real basis for disagreement and intrinsic valuing would pose no threat of relativism.

Hume begins his essay by remarking on the great variety of taste in the world. This fact has been the most powerful support that the proponents of relativism have been able to put forth and the greatest stumbling block for the nonrelativists. But what both relativists and nonrelativists have failed to notice is what underlies the great diversity of taste—the great variety of artistic values and disvalues to which taste can react. A great deal of the great variety of taste, as Hume ultimately concludes, is not something to be explained away but something to be explained by the great variety of artistic values.

Consider the implications of the cases of blameless disagreement that Hume mentions at the end of his essay. In these cases persons value different properties differently—one person, for example, values "conciseness and energy" more highly than "a copious, rich, and harmonious expression," and another person values in the reverse way—*but each property has positive aesthetic polarity.* In such cases, the disagreeing persons find each of the properties in question valuable but disagree about the relative valuableness of the properties. If given a chance to experience two works of art, Jones would value the concise one higher than the copious one and Smith would value them the other way around, but both Jones and Smith value both properties positively. Thus, it is worth noting that the relativism entailed by the blameless cases mentioned at the end of Hume's essay poses no threat to the Sibley test of aesthetic polarity adopted in Chapter Five because Hume's view does not assert that in the cases of blameless diversity one person claims positive aesthetic polarity for a property and another claims negative aesthetic polarity for the same property. Someone's inability to intelligibly say, *tout court,* "This work lacks value because it is concise and energetic (or copious and rich or the like)" functions as a universalistic test of positive polarity. In these kinds of cases everyone agrees that the properties in question have positive aesthetic polarity (or, in the reverse cases, have negative aesthetic polarity).

When, in connection with the cases of blameless diversity over the ranking of different positive aesthetic properties, Hume asserts that "we seek in vain for a standard," he means that there is no critical principle that will resolve such disagreements. But he cannot mean that no standards or principles are involved in such situations. What the blamelessly differing parties disagree about is the relative value of different positive aesthetic properties. But all parties *agree* that the aesthetic properties involved in the dispute are positively valuable. All parties would agree that, for example, "Conciseness in a work of art (in isolation from other properties) always has some value" and "Copious and harmonious expression in a work of art (in isolation from other properties) always has some value." There is, therefore, no relativism here insofar as the value of the properties themselves are concerned. The kind of relativism entailed by the cases of blameless diversity cited by Hume is of a limited sort involving only value rankings; Hume's relativism just denies that there is a principle that can resolve a dispute over the different value rankings of properties, but it does not deny that there are weak principles embodying each of the properties that form the basis of the dispute. Hume's relativism might be called "ranking relativism."

A distinction must be drawn between different kinds of principles: principles of the kind such as "Conciseness in a work of art (in isolation from other properties) is always valuable" and principles of a kind that would resolve disagreements over value rankings. The Hutchesonian principle "Uniformity in variety in a work of art is always valuable (and the only possible value)" is designed to be a principle that resolves disagreements over value rankings. This principle (together with the assumption that more is better) will always in principle resolve any dispute about the relative value of works of art because in principle it is always possible to discover which work has the most uniformity in variety. Hume, by the way, agrees with Hutcheson that uniformity in variety is always a value in a work of art (in his essay he mentions unity many times as a merit and variety several times as a merit), but he clearly disagrees that uniformity in variety is the only possible artistic value. Hume, thus, is implicitly denying that there is any principle that will in principle resolve disputes of the blameless kind, that is, disputes that do not derive from physical defect, prejudice, and the like. Hume's claim in effect is that there are *many* principles, and that because there are many principles none can function as the supreme commander as desired by Hutcheson (and Kant).

If Hume's cases of blameless diversity pose no threat to the Sibley test of aesthetic polarity, there are other blameless cases that do. Consider garishness. Assuming that most people would find a particular object's garishness distasteful, it nevertheless seems possible that in a given case someone might intrinsically value the experience of the object's garishness. I do not have in mind the kind of case in which one person finds an object garish and another person finds it colorful, which is a different situation. I also do not have in mind the kind of case in which, say, the garishness of a stage character's clothing is valued because it suits the character's personality; in this kind of case the garishness is swallowed up by an overall unity. I am considering the case in which the parties agree that an object is garish but react to it in opposite ways. The kind of situation I do have in mind is that in which one person says, "I find the garish combination of colors in the painting distasteful," but another person says, "Oh, I don't know, I agree that it is garish, but in this particular case I find its garishness rather charming." This kind of case does pose a threat to the Sibley test of aesthetic polarity because, assuming that most persons would find it unintelligible to say *tout court,* "This work has value because it is garish," it still seems possible that someone could find it intelligible to say the same thing.

The kind of case I have just been considering clearly shows that the Sibley test of aesthetic polarity is not simply a linguistic test, but that the test ultimately depends on what people actually value. It seems reasonable to think that people might in some cases disagree about the aesthetic polarity of garishness. It seems less likely that people could disagree about gracefulness, but I could be wrong. It seems impossible to me that people could disagree about the aesthetic polarity of unity; unity is so fundamental. The possibility of disagreement over the aesthetic polarity of garishness (or any other aesthetic characteristic) introduces a deeper kind of relativism than Hume's ranking variety. Hume's relativism does not threaten principles at all, only rankings, but what may be called "aesthetic polarity relativism" has the potential for undercutting principles.

The principle "Unity in a work of art (in isolation from other properties) is always valuable" is a universal principle, that is, one that is so secure that it can be cited in critical justification without fear of disagreement. Unity, which is valued by everyone, is not subject to aesthetic polarity relativism. It seems more than likely that "Gracefulness in a work of art (in isolation from other properties) is always valuable" is also a universal principle, but that is not certain. "Garishness in a work of art (in isolation from other properties) is always disvaluable" is not a universal principle; it is one that must be used with some caution.

There are, then, many critical principles. Some principles are clearly universal, involving properties the experience of which every-one always intrinsically values. Many principles appear to be univer-sal and of these no doubt many are. To speak of universal principles is to deny aesthetic polarity relativism in the case of certain proper-ties. Some principles that appear to be universal may not in fact be so. And some principles are not universal—for example, the tradi-tionally negative principle involving garishness. Such nonuniversal principles may function universally within a limited domain, for example, the domain within which everyone intrinsically disvalues cases of garishness. To speak of principles that function in domains of less than everyone is to admit to aesthetic polarity relativism in the case of certain properties.

Thus, for Hume and for the view being developed here, there can-not be, as Hutcheson would have it, a single standard of taste cover-ing all cases, a standard that justifies a qualified judge's speaking with a universal voice to coerce every differing artistic evaluation. The situation, according to Hume and the view being developed here, contrasts strongly with Hutcheson's view. For Hutcheson, there is a single standard of taste that ranges over human beings for the property uniformity in variety. But for Hume and the ampli-fied, compromise view, things are just not that simple; that is, these views both affirm ranking relativism. In addition, although it is not clear that Hume would agree, the amplified, compromise view also embraces aesthetic polarity relativism for many properties.

The amplified, compromise view does not quite fit any of the three instrumentalist theory-types outlined in Chapter One. It comes closest to theory-type 5, which is the view that

5. Works of art are valuable because they can be the instrumental source of a valuable experience that in turn is valuable because the experience or an element of it is intrinsically valued by some person or persons.

The referent-centered cognitive value acknowledged by the view being developed in this book does not fit into theory-type 5, which speaks only of properties that are intrinsically valuable (and by implication of properties that are intrinsically disvaluable). Consequently, a fourth instrumentalist theory-type must be formulated to accommodate the amplified, compromise view.

8. Works of art are valuable because they can be the instrumental source of a valuable experience that in turn is valuable because the experience or an element of it is intrinsically valued by some person or persons and/or because the experience or an element of it is of a representational feature of art that refers to a valued thing.

CHAPTER NINE

Comparison and Specificity: Vermazen and Urmson

I shall now sum up the content of the amplified, compromise view as it has been developed to this point. By the end of Chapter Five, I had concluded that definitions of primary positive and negative criteria of aesthetic value can be formulated. Since Beardsley's distinction between primary and secondary criteria has been abandoned, it is unnecessary to specify *primary* for these definitions. These definitions run as follows:

> A property is a positive criterion of aesthetic value if it is a property of a work of art and if in isolation from other properties it is valuable.

> A property is a negative criterion of aesthetic value if it is a property of a work of art and if in isolation from other properties it is disvaluable. ("Disvaluable" means "lacking in value.")

The definition of "positive criteria" and "negative criteria" of *aesthetic* value, derived from Beardsley, must be reformulated as criteria of *artistic* value, because aesthetic value is only one kind of value that art can have. The definitions must read as follows:

A property is a positive criterion of *artistic* value if it is a property of a work of art and in isolation from other properties it is valuable.

A property is a negative criterion of *artistic* value if it is a property of a work of art and in isolation from other properties it is disvaluable.

Properties that satisfy these definitions are the bases for weak sufficiency principles, for example:

Unity in a work of art (in isolation from the other properties of the work) is always valuable.

Elegance in a work of art (in isolation from the other properties of the work) is always valuable. [This principle may be one of limited scope.]

Garishness in a work of art (in isolation from the other properties of the work) is always disvaluable. [This principle is, I believe, of limited scope.]

Standard properties that are valuable (or disvaluable) are the bases for weak necessity principles, for example:

A valuable work of art is always unified.

As noted above, properties other than aesthetic properties can be of artistic value or disvalue. These other valuable or disvaluable properties are cognitive properties. There are three kinds of cognitive value or disvalue that works of art can have: (1) imitative cognitive value, (2) supportive cognitive value, and (3) referent-centered cognitive value.

The first kind of cognitive value is essentially the value associated with the imitation theory of art, namely, the value that art can have because it is true to actuality in some respect or true to a prior and independently established fictional object in some respect or because a true proposition is asserted by means of it. Imitative cognitive value yields such principles as the following:

Truth to actuality in some respect in a work of art (in isolation from the other properties of the work) is always valuable.

Asserting a true proposition by means of a work of art (in isolation from the other properties of the work) is always valuable.

The third kind of cognitive artistic value or disvalue (referent-centered) yields the principles:

The representation in works of art of anything valuable (in isolation from the other properties of the work) is always valuable.

The representation in works of art of anything disvaluable (in isolation from the other properties of the work) is always disvaluable.

Since there are so many valuable and disvaluable things—moral, cultural, and the like—these last two principles can be used with a great variety of works of art. In considering the four principles just above, one must remember that "valuable" and "disvaluable" are weak predicates, so that the presence of a property mentioned in these principles does not guarantee that a work having it is good or even that such a work has very much value (or disvalue) at all.

Supportive cognitive features do not yield principles directly in the way that the other two kinds of cognitive features do, because their function is to support aesthetic properties. The aesthetic properties, however, do yield principles.

Each of the principles mentioned above is a weak principle, so that when it is applied to a work of art that it fits, the conclusion that results must be the weak conclusion that the work in question just has some value. The more valuable properties a work has, the more value it will have, unless some of its properties do not work well together. The failure of otherwise valuable properties to work well together is a difficulty often cited by critics.

An example of a critical argument using such principles runs as follows:

1. Elegance in a work of art (in isolation from the other properties of the work) is always valuable.

2. This work of art has the property of elegance in some degree.

3. Unity in a work of art (in isolation from the other properties of the work) is always valuable.

4. This work of art has the property of unity in some degree.

5. Truth to actuality in some respect in a work of art (in isolation from other properties of the work) is always valuable.

6. This work of art is true to actuality in some degree.

7. The valuable properties of this work of art work well together and do not detract from one another.

8. Therefore, this work of art is valuable in some degree.

The conclusion is a weak one—too weak to be of interest, some might say. Suppose in this case that the premises that describe the work can be strengthened so that they assert that the work is elegant in high degree, unified in high degree, true to actuality in high degree, and that these valuable properties work well together. The conclusion will still have to be the same weak one as before because, although the premises describing the work have been strengthened, the principles that they connect with have remained the same. I do not see any way of getting strong premises or even of strengthening the weak principles to make them less weak.

How, then, is it possible to get strong, specific conclusions about works of art? With this query, I return to the question with which Ziff and Beardsley were centrally concerned—the theoretical account of strong or specific evaluations of art, that is, the question of how to distinguish bad art, mediocre art, good art, and the like from one another. Such specific evaluations must, of course, take place within the boundaries imposed by the various types of relativism. For example, if Jones blamelessly values conciseness in works of art highly and Smith blamelessly values it lowly—that is, they value-rank the property differently—then this fact may prevent their agreement on a specific evaluation of a work of art that has this property. Despite their disagreement over the ranking of a property, they may nevertheless agree on a specific evaluation of a work with that property because works of art typically have *many* value properties and their underlying blameless disagreement over conciseness or any other particular property may not make enough difference to make a difference in their overall evaluations. Similarly, if Jones and Smith blamelessly disagree over the aesthetic or artistic polarity of a property in the case of given work of art, this fact lowers the probability that they will agree on a specific evaluation of a work with that property. Agreement on a specific evaluation is not, of course, ruled out in a given case involving disagreement over polarity for the same reason cited above in connection with disagreement over the ranking of a particular property: works of art typically have many value properties and the disagreement over the polarity of one property may not make enough difference to make a difference in the overall evaluations of two parties to such a disagreement.

Before addressing the question of specific evaluations and by way of preparing the way for such a discussion, I shall focus on the problem of making evaluative comparisons of works of art—a problem that philosophers have been concerned with for a very long time. Making evaluative comparisons or rankings of works of art requires that there be a measure of something that the works of art have in common. An example of an evaluational theory that makes evaluational comparisons a straight-forward matter is the theory that I called "the objective intrinsic theory" in Chapter One. There I formulated the theory-type of this theory as follows:

> Works of art are valuable because they possess the one and only objective intrinsic value property in some degree.

In the case of this theory, the intrinsic value property is beauty. Given that one can assess the degree of beauty of works of art, one can make evaluational comparisons of works of art quite easily. The structure of such comparisons would be similar to that of comparing the weights of pieces of meat at the supermarket.

Beardsley's instrumentalist theory also allows for straight-forward evaluational comparisons of works of art. This is most easily seen from a consideration of his definition of "aesthetic value."

> "X has aesthetic value" means "X has the capacity to produce an aesthetic experience of fairly great magnitude (such an experience having value)."

This definition needs to be tidied up a bit in order to avoid Beardsley's confusion of equating the specific evaluation of "good aesthetic object" with the general evaluation of "having aesthetic value"—a difficulty noted and commented on in Chapter Four. The definition should read:

> "X has aesthetic value" means "X has the capacity to produce an aesthetic experience of *some* magnitude (such an experience having value)."

On Beardsley's theory, a work of art has the capacity to produce an aesthetic experience of some magnitude or other. Works of art can, therefore, be compared and ranked according to their capacity for producing magnitudes of aesthetic experience. A work that produces an aesthetic experience of a greater magnitude is better than one that produces an aesthetic experience of a lesser magnitude.

Unfortunately, neither the objective intrinsic theory nor Beardsley's theory is an adequate theory, and the amplified, compromise theory makes evaluative comparisons of works of art a more complicated matter.

What I shall say on the topic of comparisons takes off from Bruce Vermazen's seminal article, "Comparing Evaluations of Works of Art."[1] Vermazen's article is of the greatest importance because it offers a fresh way of looking at the comparing of works of art. He shows in a clear and penetrating way why such comparisons can be so difficult. He begins by taking for granted what I have been arguing for in this book—that the value of works of art derives from valuable properties of art *and* that there are many different valuable artistic properties. By the way, Vermazen, so far as I can tell from his article, is concerned only with the aesthetic properties of works of art. Vermazen embeds what he takes for granted in the first two of three theses he formulates.

Thesis 1: Some aspects [properties] of works of art are valued independently of their relations to other aspects of the work.[2]

In addition to independently valued properties that Vermazen here characterizes, there are, he asserts, *dependently* valued properties that are properties that are valued because of the way they interact with other properties of a work of art. I think it may be added that in order for a property to be dependently valued it must ultimately be involved in producing an independently valued property. Incidentally, it is possible for a property to be independently valued and dependently valued at the same time. What Vermazen calls independently valued properties are identical with the properties I am calling positive criteria of artistic value. He does not discuss independently disvaluable properties, but they pose no problem for his view. Dependently valued properties are identical with what I, following Sibley, have characterized as properties that through interaction contribute to artistic value; such properties may have artistic polarity or may be neutral.

> Thesis 2: Works of art nearly always have at least two aspects [properties] that are independently valued.[3]

Vermazen does not deny that some works may have only one independently valued property, but such works would be rare if they exist at all and are not typical works of art. By the way, in this chapter, I frequently use Vermazen's terminology "independently valued properties." This terminology may suggest to some that it is aesthetic properties themselves rather than the experiences of them that are intrinsically valued. "Independently valuable properties" is a better way of speaking because it does not suggest that the properties themselves are intrinsically valued; that is, "independently valuable properties" indicates that the properties are valuable because the experiences of them are valued.

The third thesis does not involve anything taken for granted but rather something for which Vermazen argues.

> Thesis 3: While it is generally possible to rank works with respect to the degree of a single independently valued property they possess, it is not generally possible to rank them with respect to the degree of two different independently valued properties.[4]

Let me illustrate the first part of Thesis 3 using that old standby unity as an example of an independently valued property. Unity is a *standard* property of works of art, that is, a property all works have in common. Works of art can, therefore, always be compared and ranked with respect to their unity. The second part of Thesis 3 can be illustrated by considering two works—a poem and a painting: both will have unity and are hence rankable with respect to unity, but how is one to compare and thus rank, say, the poem's subtle meter against the painting's brilliant color? Meter and color are such different things that it does not appear to make sense to try to compare and rank them. There are, then, many, many independently valued properties that works can and do have that are not universally shared. Thus, of half a dozen randomly selected works of art, one work might have independently valued properties A,B,C,D,E, a second work might have A,B,C,F,G, a third properties A,B,F,H,I, a fourth properties A,B,H,J,L, a fifth properties A,B,M,N,O, and a sixth A,B,P,Q,R. The comparison of these works is facilitated if their abstract descriptions are placed in a tabular form (Figure 14). In

A, B, C, D, E
A, B, C, F, G
A, B, F, H, I
A, B, H, J, L
A, B, M, N, O
A, B, P, Q, R

FIGURE 14

this abstract example, the six works have two independently valued properties in common; let one of the two be a standard property and the other be an independently valued property that the six works just happen to have in common. The six works can be compared with respect to each of the two properties they have in common. Comparisons among the overall values of the six works themselves, however, will be impossible because the overall value of each work is made up of such different sets of valuable properties.

Vermazen admits, as perhaps he should, that there may be cases in which two different properties can be ranked against one another. Examples would be when, say, a poem's subtle meter and a painting's brilliant color seem roughly to balance one another, or when one property is present in very high degree and the other only in very low degree.[5] Occasionally rankable pairs of different properties will not, however, affect the great bulk of the cases.

Even in cases in which works of art have exactly the same independently valued properties, comparisons will not always be possible. Consider the case of a class of works that share the same three independently valued properties and have only these three valuable properties—the properties of A, B, and C. The ranks of these three individual properties can be represented by numbers with the higher numbers representing higher ranks. Thus, $(A3,B1,C2)$ would be a work with a relatively high rank for A, a low rank for B, and a middling rank for C. In cases of works in which the rankings are the same for each property—for example, the pair $(A2,B2,C2)$ and $(A2,B2,C2)$—comparison is obviously possible and the conclusion is that the two works are of equal value. In cases of pairs of works in which the ranking for each of the properties of the first work is greater than the ranking of the corresponding property of the second work—for example, the pair $(A3,B2,C2)$ and $(A2,B1,C1)$ —comparison is also obviously possible and the conclusion is that the first work is better than the second. (I am ignoring for the time being the possibility of interaction of independently valued properties.) Vermazen formulates the following general condition for a work's being better than another work when the two share the same independently valued properties:

> If the numerical value of each property of the first work is equal to or greater than the numerical value of the corresponding property of the second work, and if the numerical value of some property of the first work is strictly greater than the value of the corresponding property of the second work, then the first work is strictly greater than the second.[6]

For example, the first work might be (A3,B2,C2) and the second work (A3,B2,C1).

But many cases are possible in which pairs of works of art with the same independently valued properties cannot be compared. For example, the pair of works with the values (A3,B2,C1) and (A1,B2, C3) cannot be compared. Each independently valued property of the first work is rankable against the corresponding property of the second work; property A of the first work is greater than property A of the second work, and property B of the first work is equal to property B of the second work, and property C of the second work is greater than property C of the first work. However, despite the fact that each property of the first work is comparable to the corresponding property in the second work, it is not possible to compare and rank the overall value of the two works.

In the discussion above, I have arbitrarily used the values 1, 2, and 3. Perhaps a scale of 1, 2, 3, 4, 5 would be better as it allows for finer discriminations—or a scale of 1 to 10. I use the 1, 2, 3 scale because it will supply enough cases to illustrate the evaluational process without multiplying the cases to the point of unwieldiness. In actual cases of evaluation, whatever scale is required to take account of the number of discriminations that can be made among the instances of a particular property must be used.

So there are two kinds of cases in which one cannot make evaluative comparisons: (1) different-properties cases—works of art that do not have exactly the same independently valued properties—and (2) same-properties cases—works of art that have exactly the same independently valued properties but where the values of the properties of the works are such that no overall comparison of them is possible.

Vermazen could have formulated, but did not bother to, a fourth thesis.

Thesis 4: It is not generally possible to rank works of art with respect to the degree of two or more independently valued properties even when the works have exactly the same independently valued properties.

Although it is not generally possible to compare the overall value of works of art with either the same or different independently valued properties, it will be possible to compare works with the same properties if the values of the properties are of the right sort. (I am still ignoring the fact that independently valued properties can sometimes interact.) One can compare a work (A,B,C) with a second work (A,B,C) with the right values if there is such a second work. And if there is no second work with the right values, it is always possible that in the future such a work will be created. Thus, every work is actually or potentially comparable to some other work. To take things a step farther, any work can be placed in a matrix of actual or possible works with the same properties (with the properties having appropriate values), so that for every work, there is an indefinitely large set of actual or possible works to which it may be compared. (Vermazen at the end of his article speaks briefly of *grouping* actual and possible works. He may have had in mind something similar to what I am calling a matrix.)[7] Thus, if one takes an actual work

work of art—(A,B,C)

it can be placed thusly in a matrix of actual or possible works:

first work of art—(A,B,C)
second work of art—(A,B,C)
third work of art—(A,B,C).

So, although every work cannot be compared to every other work, every work can be placed in a matrix or set of actual or possible works that share its independently valued properties. Not every work in such a matrix is comparable to every other work in the matrix, and it cannot be known which work can be compared to which

168

other work until the value rankings of the independently valued properties are known. When the values of the independently valued properties are known, what may be called a "comparison matrix" can be constructed.

Consider now an example of a same-properties pair that cannot be compared:

$$(A3,B2,C1) \text{ and } (A1,B2,C3).$$

Both of these works can, as any work of art can, become the *base* work of their own *minimal* comparison matrix, which consists of the base work and all possible works that are better or worse than the base work. The base work is placed in the matrix so that the works above it are better than it is and the works below it are worse than it is. There may be actual works with the properties and values of some or all of the possible works in the matrix, so that a given minimal comparison matrix may be constituted in three ways: (1) it may consist of the base work plus possible works only, (2) it may consist of the base work plus actual and possible works, or (3) it may consist of the base work plus other actual works only. I construct in Figure 15 a comparison matrix with (A1,B2,C3) as the base work

$$(3,3,3)$$
$$(3,2,3) - (2,3,3)$$
$$(2,2,3) - (1,3,3)$$
$$^{*}(1,2,3)^{*}$$
$$(1,2,2) - (1,1,3)$$
$$(1,2,1) - (1,1,2)$$
$$(1,1,1)$$

FIGURE 15

and in doing so omit the property letter designations in order to simplify matters. Thus, each particular set of values, for example, (2,2,3), represents an actual or possible work of art. The base work is marked by asterisks on each side of it. (Note that many possible works with exactly the same properties are not in the matrix because they are not comparable to the base work. For example, (3,3,2) is not in the matrix.) Thus, any actual work, although there will be many works to which it cannot be compared, can always be placed within its own minimal comparison matrix of works to which it can be compared. Such a minimal comparison matrix will contain actual or possible works that range from a work at the top of the matrix with all its independently valued properties at the maximum to a work at the bottom with all its independently valued properties at the minimum. Those works paired with a dash in the matrix, for example, (3,2,3)—(2,3,3), cannot be compared to one another, but each work in the matrix can be compared to the base work and to any work on its side of the matrix above or below it as well as to some works on the other side of the matrix.

A minimal comparison matrix is one in which each possible slot is filled by an actual or possible work of art. An *actual* comparison matrix for any actual work of art may in many cases be larger than a minimal one because it is possible that there will be more than one actual work of art with a particular set of values. An actual comparison matrix for a base work with the values (1,2,3) might look something like Figure 16. The base work's minimal comparison

$$
\begin{array}{ccc}
\vdots & & \vdots \\
\vdots & (3,3,3) & \vdots \ (3,3,3) \\
(2,3,3)-(3,2,3) & \vdots \ (3,2,3)-(2,3,3) & \vdots \ (3,2,3)-(3,2,3) \\
\vdots & (2,2,3)-(1,3,3) & \vdots \ (2,2,3) \\
\vdots & {}^{*}(1,2,3)^{*} & \vdots \ (1,2,3) \\
(1,2,2) & \vdots \ (1,2,2)-(1,1,3) & \vdots \ (1,2,2)-(1,1,3) \\
\vdots & (1,2,1)-(1,1,2) & \vdots \ (1,2,1)-(1,1,2) \\
\vdots & (1,1,1) & \vdots \\
\vdots & & \vdots
\end{array}
$$

FIGURE 16

matrix is contained within the actual comparison matrix and is the set of works in the middle enclosed by the two columns of dots; this minimal matrix may consist wholly of actual works, or it, with the exception of the base work, may consist wholly of possible works, or it may consist of a mixture of actual and possible works. In this example of a minimal matrix there are five actual or possible works better than the base work and five works worse than it. In this example of an actual matrix there are eleven actual or possible works better than the work being compared, ten actual or possible works worse than it, and one actual work that has the same value. Of course, many works in an actual matrix will not be comparable to other works in it, but every work in the matrix will be comparable to the base work.

An important question unbroached as yet is, How does one assign numerical values to the instances of properties of works of art? It is relatively easy to establish greater-thanness, lesser-thanness, or equality between pairs of instances of the same property; one experiences the two instances of the property in two different works and estimates that one instance is greater or less than the other or that the two instances are equal to one another. If one assumes a 1,2,3 scale and discovers that one instance of a property is greater than a second and the second greater than a third, then the scale is filled out and the first instance must be assigned the value 3, the second the value 2, and the third the value 1. This will do until one discovers an instance of the property greater than the first instance or less than the third instance, or one that falls between one of the three original instances. These further and different instances show that a larger and more discriminating scale is needed. In general, the scale to be used for a given property will be dictated by the discriminations that can be made among instances of that property. One property might require a 1,2,3 scale, another a 1,2,3,4,5 scale, a third a 1 to 10 scale, and so on. Thus, each of the properties of a given work of art might be ranked on a different scale. For example, a work might have a property A that requires a five-point scale, a property B that requires a four-point scale, and a property C that requires a three-point scale. A work (A_5, B_3, C_2) would have the minimum comparison matrix shown in Figure 17.

$$(5,4,3)$$
$$(5,4,2)$$
$$*(5,3,2)*$$

(5,3,1)	(4,3,2)	(3,3,2)	(2,3,2)	(1,3,2)
(5,2,1)	(4,2,1)	(3,2,2)	(2,2,2)	(1,2,2)
(5,1,1)	(3,2,1)			(1,1,2)
(4,1,1)	(2,2,1)			
(3,1,1)	(1,2,1)			
(2,1,1)				
(1,1,1)				

FIGURE 17

(By the way, numerical values are used only to indicate relative rankings: for example, the fact that a work merits a three-point ranking for, say, unity does not mean that it has three times as much unity as a work that merits only a one-point ranking.)

Thus far, the sample matrices I have constructed have involved only positive independently valuable properties, but works of art sometimes have negative independently disvaluable properties. Suppose, for example, there is a work that has two positive properties, say, unity and complexity, and one negative property, say, garishness. The values of unity and complexity can be represented in the same way that the values of positive properties have been represented, and the values of negative properties can be represented by negative numbers. Assuming a three-point scale for each of the three properties with unity first, garishness in the middle, and complexity third, the minimal comparison matrix shown in Figure 18 can be constructed for the work being imagined.

$$(3,-1,3)$$
$$(3,-2,3)—(2,-1,3)$$
$$(2,-2,3)—(1,-1,3)$$
$$*(1,-2,3)*$$
$$(1,-2,2)—(1,-3,3)$$
$$(1,-2,1)—(1,-3,2)$$
$$(1,-3,1)$$

FIGURE 18

As I noted twice earlier in this chapter, I have been ignoring the fact that the independently valuable properties of works of art can sometimes interact. I have constructed comparison matrices as if such properties are always also independent in the sense that they never interact. But when independently valuable properties interact within a work of art, the overall value of the work will be different from the simple "sum" of the work's independently valuable properties—greater if they interact positively and less if they interact negatively. Two works with the same independently valuable properties with the same rankings—for example, (A_3, B_2, C_1) and (A_3, B_2, C_1) —would not be of equal overall value if, say, properties A and B in the first work interact positively but in the second work interact negatively or just do not interact. The taking into account of the interaction of independently valuable properties, as must be done, threatens to undermine the use of comparison matrices. Suppose, for example, that in a work of art (A_3, B_2, C_2) properties A and B interact positively. If the work is represented as (A_3 interacts positively B_2, C_2), it is not clear how one would enter it in the kind of matrices developed earlier. Since in this case the positive interaction causes the value of (A_3 interacts positively B_2) to be greater than (A_3 not interacting with B_2), some way to represent this must be found that will fit into a comparison matrix. Since A, B, and C are all independently valued properties, each must be allowed to appear with its value represented. The value that emerges from the interaction of A and B can be represented as AB with whatever value is appropriate assigned to it. Thus, in a given case of interaction, (A3 interacting positively B2,C2) might be represented as (A3,B2,AB2,C2). Of course, instances of (A,B,C) and (A,B,AB,C) cannot appear in the same matrix because they do not have the same properties, but that is no problem because each work can generate its own comparison matrix.

The account of comparison matrices given thus far is unable to provide a way for making a comparison of a kind that critics often make. For example, a critic might say quite justifiably that *The Adventures of Huckleberry Finn* is better than *The Adventures of Tom Sawyer* because the former confronts the issue of slavery and the latter does not. Let us assume that, except for the moral property of confronting slavery, the two novels have exactly the same evaluative properties with exactly the same values. Thus, our critic would be comparing two works that do not share all the same properties. This case can be fitted into the matrix scheme by assigning *The Adventures of Tom Sawyer* a zero value for the property of confronting slavery. Thus, if A and B are the properties that the two works *clearly* share, then C can be the moral property of confronting slavery. *The Adventures of Huckleberry Finn* will have property C to a value of, say, 3 and *The Adventures of Tom Sawyer* will have C to a value of 0. The comparison between the two novels can be made as follows:

> *The Adventures of Huckleberry Finn*—(A3,B2, C3)
> *The Adventures of Tom Sawyer*—(A3,B2, C0)

A minimal comparison matrix with *The Adventures of Huckleberry Finn* as the base work and *The Adventures of Tom Sawyer* marked with one asterisk would look like Figure 19. How far the assigning of zero values can be taken to facilitate the comparison of works of art is a matter of judgment.

It is clear enough how aesthetic properties have values that fit

$$(3,3,3)$$
$$*(3,2,3)*$$
$$(3,2,2) — (3,1,3)$$
$$(3,2,1) — (3,1,2)$$
$$*(3,2,0) — (3,1,1)$$
$$(3,1,0)$$
$$(3,0,0)$$
$$(2,0,0)$$
$$(1,0,0)$$
$$(0,0,0)$$

FIGURE 19

into comparison matrices; unity, complexity, gracefulness, garishness, and the like can vary by degrees and have different values in different works. It may not be so clear how cognitive properties can be fitted into such matrices. Supportive cognitive properties are, of course, no problem because they merely serve to support aesthetic properties.

Imitative cognitive properties come in two varieties: the kind involving truth to actuality and the kind involving the assertion of truth or falsity. A work of art's truth to actuality can vary from completely true to completely false to actuality. So insofar as the first kind of imitative cognitive property is concerned, it is not significantly different from an aesthetic property. On the other hand, a proposition's being asserted by means of a work at least appears to be different. A proposition will either be true or false, so that it appears every true proposition should have, say, a value of 1 and every false proposition should have, say, a value of 0. This two-value scale will work for comparison matrices all right, but a more accurate account of how criticism actually works will involve a larger scale in which the highest value is assigned to true propositions and values are assigned to false propositions in proportion to how closely they approximate the truth.

Referent-centered cognitive properties are of only one type but involve reference to indefinitely many things. The values of such cognitive properties will vary according to the values of their referents. For purposes of comparison, the referent-centered properties of two works will have to be characterizable in the same way, for example, as both references to Napoleon, as both references to military leaders (when one refers to Napoleon and one refers to Wellington), and the like. Whenever two works refer to the same individual or thing, the referent-centered value of the two works will be the same insofar as it derives from that one individual or thing.

As the scales for properties get larger, the matrices get more complicated and thus awkward to construct. Since the matrices are used in order to see how a particular, actual work compares to all possible works with the same properties, one can achieve approximately the same comparison by placing a base work in a matrix that consists of its being embedded in representations of the relevant scales. For example, the same work used above—(A5,B3,C2), which requires a five-point scale, a four-point scale, and a three-point scale—can be placed in a simplified matrix (Figure 20). This matrix gives a sense

$$4\ 3$$
$$*(5,3,2)*$$
$$4\ 2\ 1$$
$$3\ 1$$
$$2$$
$$1$$

FIGURE 20

of how the actual work compares to what is possible for a work with these properties. It shows that for (A5,B3,C2) it is possible for only a few works with the same properties to rank higher and for a great many works over an extended range to rank lower. Of course, it is always possible that we will discover that, say, property A requires a more discriminating scale because a work is created that requires us to rank its property A as a 6. In such a case, our earlier assumption about what was possible was mistaken, although it was a reasonable assumption given our then current information.

Once works are placed within matrices that show where they rank with regard to all possibilities for their particular properties, it is a short step to see how specific evaluations of them can be arrived at.

J. O. Urmson's article "On Grading" is an extremely useful guide in thinking about the topic of the evaluational grading of art.[8] We use evaluational or grading schemes in a great variety of situations. At the beginning of his article Urmson considers how one might grade the apples from a tree in one's yard. The tree will produce many more apples than a family can use during the time that the apples ripen. He envisages a three-place grading scheme:

The really good apples,
The not so good but edible apples,
The throw outs.

The point of the grading scheme is to sort the apples so that they can be used. Urmson suggests the following uses: the top class is for storing or sale; the middle class is for immediate use or sale at a lower price; and the bottom class is for throwing away or feeding to pigs. This simple scheme is geared to dealing with a backyard apple tree that receives minimal spraying or other care. Professional apple growers who take better care of their trees and have a larger market need a more refined scheme with more places. Urmson discusses only the two top grades that professional growers use—Super Grade and Extra Fancy Grade—but the complete scale must run to at least five or six places. Although there are variations, we use the following sort of scale to grade students on everything from mathematics to deportment:

Excellent
Good
Fair
Poor
Fail

Apples and students are graded according to how they rank on standard valued properties: for apples, color, firmness, lack of worminess, and the like; for students, mathematics problems done correctly, obedience, and the like. A Super Grade Red Delicious apple is no doubt one that ranks at the very top for all of its standard valued properties—dark red, firm but not hard, no worm holes, and the like. In other words, a Super Grade Red Delicious apple is one that sits atop a matrix of standard value features for Red Delicious apples.

It is possible to grade works of art in a similar manner, although of course works of art, unlike apples, will have many nonstandard independently valued properties. Consider again the minimal comparison matrix of the work (A1,B2,C3), or consider the work's simplified matrix (Figure 21). In the case of either matrix the base work

$$(3,3,3)$$
$$(3,2,3) - (2,2,3) \qquad 3$$
$$(2,2,3) - (1,3,3) \qquad 2 \ 3$$
$$*(1,2,3)* \qquad\qquad *(1,2,3)*$$
$$(1,2,2) - (1,1,3) \qquad 1 \ 2$$
$$(1,2,1) - (1,1,2) \qquad 1$$
$$(1,1,1)$$

FIGURE 21

178

is exactly in the middle of the matrix, which indicates that the base work is a fair or middling work. An excellent work is one that sits at the top of its matrix. A good work is one which sits high in the matrix but not at the top. A poor work falls low in the matrix but not at the bottom. And a bad work falls at or very near the bottom of its matrix. Of course, our estimate of the ranking of a given work may alter over time because, as noted a few pages back, the creation of new works may reveal to us that higher ranks for particular properties are possible. If this occurs, then the relative position of the given work may change and may require a different specific evaluation. (As noted earlier, Vermazen makes remarks that indicate that he may have had in mind something similar to my notion of a comparison matrix. Similarly, he also concludes that the place a work of art has in a grouping of conceivable works with the same properties correlates with the work's specific value ranking.)[9]

I have just said that it is *possible* to grade works of art by their positions in comparison matrices. Is there a better or even *any* other way to evaluate them specifically? There is not, I believe, any other way to arrive at specific evaluations of works of art. Beardsley's theory is the only plausible alternative, and it is not, I have argued, an acceptable theory. If Beardsley's theory were acceptable, it would be preferred by more philosophers than the theory being developed here because it tries to achieve what philosophers have traditionally wished to realize with regard to the theory of evaluational criticism. Consider for a moment some aspects of his theory and how they differ from comparable aspects of the theory being developed here.

Beardsley's theory purports to be able to compare every work of art with every other work of art by means of each work's capacity to produce aesthetic experience. This capacity is what works of art all have in common. On my view, a work of art can be compared only to those actual or possible works that constitute its actual comparison matrix. For Beardsley's theory there is only *one* comparison matrix for *all* works of art, and it is on the basis of one very complex valuable property—the capacity to produce aesthetic experience—that the matrix is built up. On my theory, there are indefinitely many comparison matrices. If it is assumed, for the purpose of illustrating the comparison matrix deriving from Beardsley's theory, that the capacity to produce aesthetic experience requires a five-point scale, then the minimal comparison matrix for a work of art with a four-point capacity will look like Figure 22. On Beardsley's view there

$$(5)$$
$$*(4)*$$
$$(3)$$
$$(2)$$
$$(1)$$

F I G U R E   2 2

will be no need to resort to comparing a work of art to possible works of art, because since there is only one matrix, there will be plenty of actual works to fill in all possible slots required for a comparison.

I would suppose that a four-point capacity to produce aesthetic experience would be a capacity to produce, to use Beardsley's phrase, "an aesthetic experience of fairly great magnitude." A work with such a capacity, on Beardsley's view, is a good work of art. On this view, to say that a work of art is a good one is to say a very great deal, namely, that it ranks very high in the *whole* class of works of art, although not at the very top of that class. Unfortunately, Beardsley's highly unified theory does not work, and we are left with a more fragmented view.

I claimed earlier that there is no better or even any other way at all to arrive at reasonable specific evaluations of works of art. But do actual critics use the method I have outlined? Of course, critics do not actually construct formal comparison matrices in their reviews and determine a work's specific evaluation according to where a work falls in its comparison matrix. But critics almost always do talk about the valuable properties of works, and they frequently compare works informally to other works that share common properties, and when they do go on to issue specific evaluations, I believe that the only thing they can be doing is estimating where a work they are talking about falls in a comparison matrix that they somewhat vaguely but not necessarily inaccurately have in mind. My remarks about comparison matrices and the places that works of art have in them is not supposed to be an exact account of what it is that critics do when they compare and evaluate works of art specifically. My remarks are a philosopher's account of the logic that underlies critics' evaluations and what such evaluations would be like if they were made as precise as they could be made. I do not wish to claim that such precise-as-can-be accounts are goals toward which critics should strive; such formally precise accounts would probably not serve the purpose of criticism as well as less precise accounts do.

At the beginning of this chapter, I summarized the amplified, compromise view as it had been developed to that point. Now, I shall summarize that summary and add a final remark.

I characterized both positive and negative criteria of *artistic* value. These criteria supply the bases of (1) many weak aesthetic sufficiency principles, (2) several weak aesthetic necessity principles, and (3) two kinds of weak cognitive sufficiency principles that involve imitative and referent-centered cognitive value. Some of the weak aesthetic sufficiency principles may be universal and some may be limited in scope.

Earlier in the book, I distinguished between strong and weak critical principles. I do not believe that this distinction had been previously noted or clearly drawn by philosophers. Because all of the principles underwritten by the amplified, compromise view are weak and because I can find no way to justify strong principles, the ways that Ziff, Beardsley, and perhaps others attempt to support specific, strong evaluations such as "X is good" and "X is bad" seem unjustified. In this final chapter, I have tried to work out a way that can account for specific evaluations but that presupposes only weak principles.

NOTES

CHAPTER TWO

1. Anthony, Earl of Shaftesbury, *Characteristics of Men, Manners, Opinions, Times* (Indianapolis: Bobbs-Merrill, 1964), vol. 1, p. 296.

2. *Ibid.*, vol. 2, p. 127.

3. *Ibid.*

4. *Ibid.*, pp. 126–127.

5. Edmund Burke, *A Philosophical Enquiry into the Origin of Our Ideas of the Sublime and Beautiful*, ed. James T. Boulton (2nd ed.; London and Notre Dame, Ind.: Notre Dame University Press, 1958), p. 91.

6. Francis Hutcheson, *An Inquiry into the Original of Our Ideas of Beauty and Virtue* (2nd ed.; London: no pub., 1726).

7. Peter Kivy, *The Seventh Sense* (New York: Burt Franklin and Co., 1976), p. 33.

8. David Hume, "Of the Standard of Taste," reprinted in *Aesthetics: A Critical Anthology*, ed. George Dickie and R. J. Sclafani (New York: St. Martin's Press, 1977), pp. 592–606.

9. *Ibid.*, p. 604.

10. *Ibid.*, p. 605.

11. Immanuel Kant, *The Critique of Judgement*, trans. J. C. Meredith (Oxford: Clarendon Press, 1928), p. 42.

12. Arthur Schopenhauer, *The World as Will and Representation*, trans. E. F. J. Payne (New York: Dover, 1969), vol. 1.

13. *Ibid.*, p. 176.

14. *Ibid.*, p. 178.

15. *Ibid.*

16. *Ibid.*, vol. 2, p. 369.

17. *Ibid.*

18. *Ibid.*, p. 370.
19. *Ibid.*, p. 373.

CHAPTER THREE

1. Paul Ziff, "Reasons in Art Criticism," in *Art and Philosophy*, ed. W. E. Kennick (2nd ed.; New York: St. Martin's Press, 1979), pp. 669–686; reprinted from *Philosophy and Education*, ed. Israel Scheffler (Boston: Allyn and Bacon, 1958), pp. 219–236.
2. Monroe Beardsley, *Aesthetics: Problems in the Philosophy of Criticism* (New York: Harcourt, Brace, and World, 1958), pp. 454–556.
3. Ziff, "Reasons in Art Criticism," p. 683.
4. *Ibid.*, p. 685.
5. *Ibid.*, p. 680.
6. William Kennick, commentary in Kennick, ed., *Art and Philosophy*, p. 726.
7. Beardsley, *Aesthetics*, p. 530; italics mine.
8. Ziff, "Reasons in Art Criticism," p. 686.
9. *Ibid.*
10. *Ibid.*, p. 684.

CHAPTER FOUR

1. Monroe Beardsley, *Aesthetics: Problems in the Philosophy of Criticism* (New York: Harcourt, Brace, and World, 1958), pp. 454–556.
2. *Ibid.*, pp. 456–457.
3. Monroe Beardsley, "In Defense of Aesthetic Value," in *Proceedings and Addresses of the American Philosophical Association* (Newark, Del.: American Philosophical Association, 1979), pp. 723–749.
4. Beardsley, *Aesthetics*, p. 528.
5. *Ibid.*, p. 529.
6. *Ibid.*, pp. 529–530.
7. Beardsley, "In Defense of Aesthetic Value," pp. 741–742.
8. See Chapter Six of this book for a discussion of Goodman's points.
9. Beardsley, "In Defense of Aesthetic Value," p. 729.

10. Beardsley, *Aesthetics*, p. 470.

11. *Ibid.*, p. 472.

12. *Ibid.*, p. 530.

13. *Ibid.*, p. 531.

14. Monroe Beardsley, "On the Generality of Critical Reasons," *Journal of Philosophy* 59 (1962): 477–486.

15. *Ibid.*, p. 485.

16. See Chapter Six for Goodman's view.

17. Robert Yanal, "Denotation and the Aesthetic Appreciation of Literature," *Journal of Aesthetics and Art Criticism* 36 (1978): 472–478.

CHAPTER FIVE

1. Monroe Beardsley, "On the Generality of Critical Reasons," *Journal of Philosophy* 59 (1962): 477–486.

2. *Ibid.*, p. 483.

3. *Ibid.*, p. 485.

4. *Ibid.*, p. 484.

5. *Ibid.*, pp. 483–484.

6. *Ibid.*, p. 485.

7. *Ibid.*, p. 486.

8. *Ibid.*

9. *Ibid.*, p. 485.

10. Frank Sibley, "General Criteria and Reasons in Aesthetics," in *Essays on Aesthetics: Perspectives on the Work of Monroe Beardsley*, ed. John Fisher (Philadelphia: Temple University Press, 1983), pp. 3–20.

11. *Ibid.*, p. 4.

12. *Ibid.*

13. *Ibid.*, p. 5.

14. *Ibid.*

15. Beardsley, "On the Generality of Critical Reasons," p. 486.

16. Sibley, "General Criteria and Reasons in Aesthetics," p. 10.

17. *Ibid.*, p. 13.

CHAPTER SIX

1. Nelson Goodman, *Languages of Art: An Approach to a Theory of Symbols* (Indianapolis and New York: Bobbs-Merrill, 1968), pp. 255–265.

2. Nelson Goodman, "When Is Art?" in *Ways of Worldmaking* (Indianapolis and Cambridge: Hackett Publishing Co., 1978), pp. 57–70.

3. Monroe Beardsley, "Languages of Art and Art Criticism," *Erkenntnis* 12 (1978): 95–118; Nelson Goodman, "Reply to Beardsley," *Erkenntnis* 12 (1978): 169–173.

4. Goodman, *Languages of Art*, p. 136.

5. Goodman, *Ways of Worldmaking*, p. 68.

6. *Ibid.*

7. *Ibid.*

8. *Ibid.*

9. Goodman, *Languages of Art*, p. 254.

10. Goodman, *Ways of Worldmaking*, pp. 68–69.

11. Goodman, *Languages of Art*, pp. 255–265.

12. *Ibid.*, p. 258.

13. Goodman, *Ways of Worldmaking*, p. 65.

14. Beardsley, "In Defense of Aesthetic Value," in *Proceedings and Addresses of the American Philosophical Association* (Newark, Del.: American Philosophical Association, 1979), p. 747.

15. Goodman, *Ways of Worldmaking*, p. 69.

CHAPTER SEVEN

1. Nicholas Wolterstorff, *Art in Action* (Grand Rapids, Mich.: William B. Eerdmans Publishing Co., 1980).

2. *Ibid.*, p. 158.

3. Monroe Beardsley, "In Defense of Aesthetic Value," in *Proceedings and Addresses of the American Philosophical Association* (Newark, Del.: American Philosophical Association, 1979), p. 729.

4. Wolterstorff, *Art in Action*, p. 158.

5. *Ibid.*, p. 157.

6. *Ibid.*, p. 159.

7. *Ibid.*

8. *Ibid.*

9. Robert Yanal, "Denotation and the Aesthetic Appreciation of Literature," *Journal of Aesthetics and Art Criticism* 36 (1978): 471–478.

10. *Ibid.*, p. 474.

11. *Ibid.*, pp. 475–476.

12. Wolterstorff, *Art in Action*, p. 159.

CHAPTER EIGHT

1. David Hume, "Of the Standard of Taste," reprinted in *Aesthetics: A Critical Anthology*, ed. George Dickie and R. J. Sclafani (New York: St. Martin's Press, 1977), p. 596.

2. *Ibid.*, p. 601.

3. *Ibid.*, pp. 601–602.

4. *Ibid.*, p. 602.

5. *Ibid.*, p. 603.

6. *Ibid.*, p. 604.

7. *Ibid.*, p. 603.

8. *Ibid.*

CHAPTER NINE

1. Bruce Vermazen, "Comparing Evaluations of Works of Art," reprinted in *Art and Philosophy*, ed. W. E. Kennick (2nd ed.; New York: St. Martin's Press, 1979), pp. 707–718. This article was originally published in the *Journal of Aesthetics and Art Criticism* 34 (1975): 7–14, but some material from the article was inadvertently left out.

2. *Ibid.*, p. 708.

3. *Ibid.*, p. 710.

4. *Ibid.*, p. 711.

5. *Ibid.*, pp. 711–712.

6. *Ibid.*, paraphrase of p. 712; I have rewritten Vermazen's passage to avoid its technical terminology.

7. *Ibid.*, p. 716.

8. J. O. Urmson, "On Grading," *Mind* 59 (1950): 145–169.

9. Vermazen, "Comparing Evaluations," pp. 716–717.

INDEX

Aesthetic and cognitive features of art, relation of, 118, 119, 120–121; experience of, 118, 119, 122–124

Aesthetic aspects of art, 13

Aesthetic-attitude theory, 33, 34

Aesthetic experience, 53–54; detachedness of, 56, 78–80, 100, 102; measurement of, 70–74; reference in, 58; standard features of, 59–60, 95, 135, 165; theory of, 54–60

Aesthetic perception, 59

Aesthetic polarity, 134, 150; -relativism, 153; Sibley test of, 93, 99, 133, 135, 150, 151, 152, 153; Ziff-Beardsley test of, 94–95, 134, 135; Ziff-Sibley test of aesthetic and/or artistic polarity, 97

Aesthetic, symptoms of the, 104, 110

Aesthetic value, criterion of, 157. *See* Primary criteria of aesthetic value; secondary criterion of aesthetic value

Affective reliability, 141, 145–154

Austen, Jane, 120, 124

Amplified compromise view, 129, 139, 140, 154; summarized, 157–161, 181

Andrews, Linda, ix

Aristotle, 15

Art, aesthetic features of, 13

Artistic value, criterion of, 158; possible theory-types of, 5–11

Beardsley, Monroe, ix, 4, 8, 13, 14, 15, 39, 43, 47, 48, 87, 88, 90, 91, 92, 93, 94, 96, 98, 99, 100, 102, 105, 107, 109, 110, 111, 112, 115, 116, 117, 118, 122, 123, 129–130, 131, 132, 133, 134, 137, 139, 140, 157, 161, 182; account of comparison of values of works of art, 162–163; aesthetic experience, later version, 56–60; compromise view of Beardsley and Sibley, 99, 101; conception of aesthetic experience, 121–122, 124; definition of "aesthetic object," 64; definition of "aesthetic value," 65; definition of "artwork," 58, 117; five symptoms of the aesthetic, 57–58; theory of art evaluation, 53–80; theory of critical generality, 81–87; theory of detachedness of aesthetic experience, 58–59; theory of evaluation and comparison of values of works of art, 179–180; Ziff-Beardsley test of aesthetic polarity, 94–95, 134, 135

Beauty and referentiality, 21–23

Blameless diversity, 146–147, 150, 151, 152, 161

Brubaker, David, ix

Budziak, Teresa, ix